Valles Caldera

PRESS   SANTA FE

Valles Caldera

A Vision for New Mexico's National Preserve

WILLIAM deBUYS   DON J. USNER

Project editor: Mary Wachs
Design and production: Deborah Flynn Post
Map: Deborah Reade
Composition: Bembo and Gill Sans
Manufactured in China
10 9 8 7 6 5 4 3 2 1

Museum of New Mexico Press
Post Office Box 2087
Santa Fe, New Mexico 87504
www.mnmpress.org

Library of Congress Cataloging-in-Publication Data
DeBuys, William Eno.
  Valles Caldera : a vision for New Mexico's national preserve / by William deBuys and Don J. Usner.
        p. cm.
   ISBN-13: 978-0-89013-493-1 (clothbound : alk. paper)
  1. Valles Caldera National Preserve (N.M.)—Pictorial works. 2. Valles Caldera National Preserve (N.M.)—Description and travel. 3.   Natural history—New Mexico—Valles Caldera. 4. Valles Caldera National Preserve (N.M.)—History. 5. Valles Caldera National Preserve (N.M.)—Management.   I. Usner, Donald J. II. Title.
   F802.S3D43 2006
   978.9'57—DC22
                                                        2006013060

Contents

ACKNOWLEDGMENTS

A definitive and thorough history of the federal acquisition of Baca Location No. 1 deserves to be written. It is a story rich in drama, irony, and intrigue. In the meantime, the partial account provided herein will perhaps suffice. No doubt it contains errors, and these are mine alone. That it does not contain more is a result of the kindness of Linda Lance, Janet Potts, Dave Sherman, Jim Snow, and Gary Ziehe, to all of whom I owe much thanks. Dinah Bear, Terry Johnson, Marty Peale, Ray Powell, and Tom Swetnam also helped to rescue the manuscript from various lapses and errors. Where their rescue was unsuccessful, the responsibility, again, is solely mine. I am grateful to each of them, as well as to the Eugene V. and Clare E. Thaw Charitable Trust, which helped to make this book possible.

I would also like to extend my thanks and best wishes to the dedicated staff of the Valles Caldera Trust, present and past, and to the fellow board members with whom I served, especially the eight good-hearted and hardworking individuals who were sworn in with me on January 10, 2001. It was an honor and a privilege to work with them in service to land as superlative as the Valles Caldera.—*WB*

I am indebted to William deBuys and his colleagues on the first board of trustees of the Valles Caldera Trust for hiring me to take photographs in the preserve. For advocating continued access and use of my photographs for preserve publications, I thank Julie Grey Pollock, former communication manager for the preserve. Others on the preserve staff also proved helpful and supportive, especially D. Rourke McDermott, preserve manager Dennis Trujillo, and former preserve director Ray Powell. On the land, ranch foreman Randy McKee provided practical guidance, and his ranch hands were equally obliging in helping me get around. To help me write photo captions, USGS research ecologist Craig Allen and Los Alamos National Laboratory geologist Steve Reneau spent hours poring over photographs, offering their insights into the landscape. Craig Martin and Bill Zeedyk also graciously provided me with useful and perceptive comments on selected photographs. Marty Peale, coordinator of the Valles Caldera Coalition, gave generously of her time and energy as she reviewed my writing and photographs. To all of these people, each one of whom has an abiding passion for the Valles Caldera, I am deeply grateful.

Additionally, I owe thanks to Jaune Evans, Tom Ribe, Christa Sadler, and Stella Usner for reading drafts of my manuscript and providing comments that corrected errors and greatly improved the writing; to Tony O'Brien and David Scheinbaum, for their help with the process of selecting photographs from a multitude of possibilities; to Brooks White, for carrying photo gear on winter trips, and Scott Swearingen for loaning me equipment; and to B. C. Rimbeaux, who flew me on spectacular flights over the caldera so I could take aerial photographs.

Most of all, thanks to my wife, Deborah, and my daughter, Jennifer, for their consistent love and support.

The Eugene V. and Clare E. Thaw Charitable Trust provided a grant in support of the writing for this project.—*DU*

The Land Alive

WILLIAM DE BUYS

Photographs by Don J. Usner

We had not seen any eagles, although that had been our purpose. The only raptor we saw all day was a peregrine falcon winging hard above the Valle Toledo with the mutilated remains of what might have been a duck dangling from its talons.

It was March, and Terry Johnson, a wildlife biologist working for the Valles Caldera Trust, wanted to know if the bald eagles that lingered along the Rio San Antonio in the fall also stopped there when they headed north in the spring. I had come along for the chance to see the remote interior of the Valles Caldera National Preserve under winter conditions, and to do so in the company of an exceptional guide. In a more typical winter we'd have had to ski or snowshoe several miles to reach the "back" of the caldera, but in 2002 so little snow had fallen that, mere days past the equinox, the roads were already clear and hard. The lack of snowpack boded ill for the landscape in numerous ways, but for the moment it made our work easy.

Most people know the Valles Caldera from the spectacular views afforded from State Route 4, which cuts across the caldera's southeast corner. If you drive, say, from Los Alamos, New Mexico, to Jemez Springs, you will cross a high mountain ridge, which is the rim of the caldera, after which you briefly descend through forest. Then suddenly, rounding a long, sweeping bend, the forest ends and the space before you bursts outward into a giant, grass-carpeted mountain bowl. The bottom of the bowl, unbroken grassland with a river meandering down its center, is easily four miles across, to say nothing of its forested sides. So abrupt is the change, so unexpected the sudden abundance of space and light and visual detail, that you are left wordless. Or you swear, invoking all the impact four letters can provide. Then you fall silent. Maybe, like many travelers, you feel a sudden need to pull over and get out of the car. You want to make sure you are seeing what you think you are seeing. A seemingly misplaced prairie lies before you, a tawny sea of grass miles deep and broad, which has been dropped into the top of a heavily forested mountain range. This stunning grassland bowl is the Valle Grande.

First-time visitors to the Valles Caldera sometimes assume that the Valle Grande *is* the caldera, but in fact the caldera, a circular basin more than twelve miles across, is many times larger than its largest valle, and the mountains that rise within it divide its internal spaces into many additional grassy bowls, or *valles*. (A *valle* is not strictly a *valley*; the Spanish term emphasizes openness, while the English denotes topography.) Generations ago, before U.S. government maps firmly established Jemez as the name of the mountain range, the people of the Rio Grande valley, looking west, called the whole range la Sierra de los Valles, and the names of its valles were a kind of roll call of the places they knew and hunted and herded in: Valle de los Posos, Valle Seco, Valle Jaramillo, Valle Santa Rosa, Valle San Antonio, Valle Toledo. Each was a sprawling, verdant, self-contained world of its own.

Narrow, trout-rich streams snake across the floors of the largest valles. These creeks form the headwaters of the Rio Jemez, and the caldera they drain is home to mountain lion, black bear, elk, mule deer, bobcat, coyote, badger, prairie dog, wild turkey, blue grouse, and more than a hundred other species of birds. The thick forests of the resurgent mountain domes are among the most productive in the Southwest. Fed by rich volcanic soils, the caldera's Douglas fir and ponderosa pine, in particular, grow to stunning size. There are strange places within the basin, too. Hot springs, sulfur baths, and bogs saturated with corrosively acidic water testify that the forces that shaped the caldera's volcanic past may be dormant but they are not absent. In the 1970s and 1980s, bulldozers carved several dozen drilling pads into canyon sides southwest of Redondo Peak as part of a failed effort to harness the geothermal resources of the caldera. Wells were drilled more than a mile into the bowels of the earth, and had the enterprise proved successful, it would

have brought several factories' worth of industrial activity into the caldera and gouged a high-voltage electrical transmission line across the tops of its central mountains. Although the wells were hot, the profits did not pencil out, and today the caldera remains a home more to leather than to steel, to elk and cattle instead of machinery, and from the top of Redondo—which at 11,254 feet towers more than half a mile above the floor of the Valle Grande—or from any other vantage, the sound you hear is the sound of silence blown in on the back of the wind, not just from the great distances that sprawl away in every direction but from the sense, which is palpable in the caldera, that time itself stretches before you as much as space does and that the eloquent silence of the land has been welling up from the eons of the past, just as you are hearing it now, since the first day of creation.

It was in the Valle Toledo and the upper Valle San Antonio that Terry and I thought we might spot eagles. The Rio San Antonio winds down the length of the former and then squeezes past an ancient volcanic cone into the latter, broadening its meanders as its volume, fed by springs and one perennial tributary, steadily increases. From first one lookout then another, always keeping a distance, Terry and I trained our binoculars on the tall conifers growing closest to the stream. Bald eagles commonly perch in such trees, where they watch for fish in the water below. We also scanned a stand of trees that Terry had identified the previous fall as the eagles' favored nighttime roost. Under the trees he'd collected numerous pellets, dense with fish bones, that the birds had egested, confirming that the fishery was part of what had attracted them to the caldera. Another fall attractant is no doubt the piles of elk guts left behind when hunters butcher their kills. Bald eagles are eager scavengers and will gorge on the entrails until they can scarcely fly.

We scanned the roost and the fishing trees in the morning, again in the warmth of midday, and also late in the afternoon as shadows lengthened and cold began to descend. No bald eagles. No golden eagles, either, although they are not uncommon in the caldera. The goldens like to perch where they can stake out a prairie dog town and keep an eye on their favorite food. But the dogs were still deep in their burrows, and the whole landscape seemed quiet and vacant and frowsy with winter sleep. Aside from the single peregrine, and several ravens and robins, we saw few birds of any kind. It was a good day in the field—we had clear weather and all the peace and solitude we could wish for—but it had been unremarkable.

Shortly after sundown, we climbed back into Terry's truck. The moon, a few days short of full, had risen low over the caldera's rim, but the land was dark, and Terry turned on the headlights as we took the road home. We forded the river where today a bridge provides a crossing and headed south across the San Antonio toward the Valle Santa Rosa. Terry turned on the heater of the truck, and soon the cab, after our long day of walking, felt warm and welcoming. We were not in a hurry, and we drove slowly—fifteen, maybe twenty miles an hour. We stared down the bright tunnel that the headlights bored into the night and listened to the hum of the engine, speaking little. Everything seemed right, yet something felt odd. I could not tell for sure but a strange shimmer appeared to hover off to the right, just outside the bright tunnel of the headlights. I stared out the side window and saw nothing—my eyes were unadjusted to the darkness. Still, there seemed to be movement in the darkness, as though flecks of moonlight were rising and falling on black waves. Terry had noticed it, too, and was casting glances to the side.

"Terry, is there something out there?"

"I don't know. Seems like maybe there is."

I rolled down my window. Cold air poured in, and I peered hard into the night. Yes, now I could see a little more. I could discern the vague outline of bodies beside us moving in the darkness, rising and falling in a rocking motion, keeping pace with the truck. The nearest were almost close enough to touch. They cantered a few arm's lengths away, on the far side of the road ditch. And beyond them, there were more, and then still more beyond those. There was no telling how far the rocking mass of bodies extended. They were like dream shapes, pitching up and down as they ran, moonlight glinting here on an eye, there on a shoulder, and there seemed to be as many of them as could fit within the limited range of my senses, which made the mass of them seem infinite, as though they stretched away into the night for as far as there was room to run. And then, separate from the drone of the truck, I began to hear a new sound. A sound of drumming. It was the sound of hooves, the hooves of a herd of elk, not pounding, because elk do not run heavily as horses do, but pattering like a steady rain on

VALLES CALDERA FROM SPACE

This photograph, taken in June 1991 from the Space Shuttle Columbia, shows the Valles Caldera and surrounding terrain, including most of the Jemez Mountains and the Pajarito Plateau. Image courtesy of the Image Science & Analysis Laboratory, NASA Johnson Space Center. (Mission STS040, Roll 614, Frame: 63.)

a canvas roof, and there seemed to be as many hooves as there are raindrops in a storm.

Terry heard them, too. He grinned and held his speed, and we listened to the drumming and watched the dim glint of moonlight on the swaying backs. And then, listening more closely, I heard another sound, a kind of fierce sighing, an in and out of many small winds—the breathing of the cantering herd.

They ran beside the truck, steady and collected, huffing easily but forcefully, like an athlete at work. I had no idea how many elk there were, how far ahead or behind or how deep into the darkness the band extended. But they kept the pace and stayed with us. Several times a shoulder or a white rump flashed at the edge of the field of our headlights, and then it vanished anew into the dark. The herd ran with us for long minutes, maybe the better part of a mile. Then suddenly it melted away, and we were alone. For me the sensation was like flying through clouds and then bursting into empty air. Now there were no drumming hooves, no heaving lungs. But then, before I finished rolling up the window, the elk were back, or they were different elk, running with us as before. They ran with us another mile. And then they were gone. And then they were back again. All along the length of the Valle Santa Rosa and across the divide into and then descending the Valle Jaramillo, we drove in and out of what seemed a restless sea of elk. By the time we reached the bottom of the Jaramillo, where it empties into the Valle Grande, the moon was high and strong enough that we could see deep into the darkness and confirm that hundreds of elk cantered and milled in the meadows on either side of the road.

We continued into the Valle Grande, circling along its edge, and it seemed we were never out of contact with bands of elk. They were streaming, band by band, out of the forests and down into the grasslands,

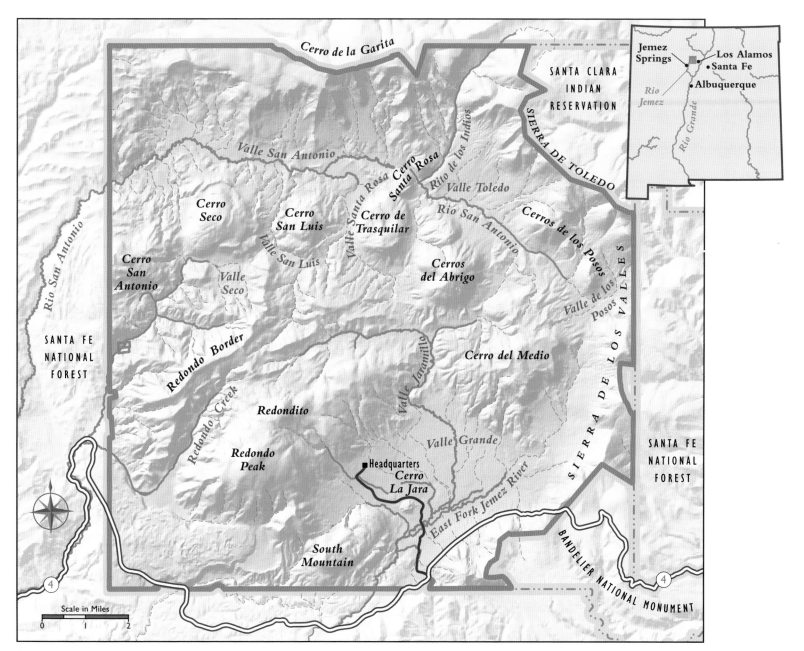

Cerro de la Garita

SANTA CLARA INDIAN RESERVATION

SIERRA DE TOLEDO

Valle San Antonio

Rito de los Indios

Cerro Santa Rosa

Valle Santa Rosa

Valle Toledo

Cerro Seco

Cerro San Luis

Cerro de Trasquilar

Rio San Antonio

Cerros de los Posos

Valle San Luis

Rio San Antonio

Cerro San Antonio

Valle Seco

Cerros del Abrigo

Valle de los Posos

SANTA FE NATIONAL FOREST

Redondo Border

Cerro del Medio

SIERRA DE LOS VALLES

Redondo Creek

Redondito

Valle Jaramillo

Redondo Peak

■ **Headquarters Cerro La Jara**

Valle Grande

SANTA FE NATIONAL FOREST

East Fork Jemez River

South Mountain

BANDELIER NATIONAL MONUMENT

④

④

Scale in Miles
0   1   2

Jemez Springs

Los Alamos
• Santa Fe

Rio Jemez

• Albuquerque

Rio Grande

GEOGRAPHIC FEATURES OF THE VALLES CALDERA

and they were so plentiful that they seemed an emanation of the land itself, a kind of living skin animated by the descent of night.

No doubt the odd behavior of the elk pacing the truck can be explained, and perhaps the explanation will even be correct. The first band that ran beside us may have been the vanguard of a larger group that intended to cross the road. They ran to get ahead of us and complete their crossing, but could not, and instead they ran parallel with us until they tired or realized in the elky depths of their minds that the truck's obstruction was temporary and they could easily cross behind. Perhaps other bands we drove beside had similar concerns. Perhaps a few (all but unheard of in New Mexico) had once been fed from trucks and thought we meant a meal. Perhaps, fresh from winter solitude and feeding now in newly collected large groups, they were jumpy and prone to run. Such explanations have the virtue of being logical, but the logic is human, not cervid, and so it is certainly incomplete. What lingers from the experience is the sense of the land's animation and abundance—Terry and I estimated we encountered more than 1,500 elk within the caldera that night—and the sense of that abundance flowing across the land as a kind of living and breathing tissue, a cloak upon the land that was as tangible as the land itself and yet also ethereal, like a spirit of the night. It was as though we had peeked behind the screen of our own senses and glimpsed a dimension of the caldera that human eyes are rarely privileged to see.

LAND OF HEART'S DESIRE

I cannot say precisely what it is about the Valles Caldera that captures people. I cannot even say what it was that captured me. Spaciousness is part of it, the pure open rolling volume of the place, which is enormous and yet self-contained and enclosed by the encircling caldera rim. When you are in the caldera, everything else you see is in it with you. It is a separate world. Pure aesthetics is another part. There must be something universal in the colors and composition of the landscape that pleases every taste: the yellow-tan flats of the grasslands stretching to the dark spruce mountainsides. And no one within the spaces of the caldera can be unmoved by the brilliance of the high-altitude light, the angled shadows of the tall pines, or the mist that rises slow and cool on wet mornings. In summer the play of color becomes even more entrancing as the tawniness of the valles breaks into a mosaic of countless soft shades of green, each variation representing different sedge and grass communities swirled together in the complexity of the bottoms. Steep cliffs and rugged canyons dominate the caldera in its southwest corner, but most of the landscape is shaped into gentle, almost female contours. It is a congeries of mounded domes and rounded lake terraces. Sharp edges are rare, and the pace of the rivers is slow and easy. Across large distances, your path unfolds before you, open and gradual. The land seems inviting. The invitation casts a spell.

The lure of the land drew in the ancestors of Jemez Pueblo, who migrated to the region hundreds of years ago and who, from the start, recognized within the caldera some of their holiest places, anchors of their universe. It had a similar effect on ancestors of today's Zia, Santa Clara, and San Ildefonso pueblos, whose attachment to the land runs deep, like a taproot of their culture. And it also entranced many others, including the descendants of Luís María Cabeza de Baca, who, in the settlement of a land grant dispute in which they claimed to have been terribly wronged, chose the caldera as the prize of their compensation.

In the earliest days of the Mexican Republic, the provincial council of Nueva Vizcaya awarded Cabeza de Baca a sprawling land grant encompassing the region around present-day Las Vegas, New Mexico. Cabeza de Baca, however, did not live to enjoy the bounty of his new kingdom, for he died in 1827 from wounds received in a fracas with Mexican soldiers. His heirs fared not much better, as Indian hostilities prevented them from permanently occupying or otherwise developing the grant. Little more than a decade later, Mexican authorities, eager to expand the effective boundaries of their territory, issued a second and overlapping grant to a hardy band of pioneers who established the town of Las Vegas and whose descendants eventually scattered homes throughout its hinterland. The heirs of Cabeza de Baca, now sometimes shortening their name to Baca, cried foul, and continued their protests even after the United States invaded Mexico in 1846 and took possession of the region. The Treaty of Guadalupe Hidalgo finalized the conquest in 1848, and not long after New Mexico was organized as a territory, the Bacas presented their grievance to U.S. authorities. Unfortunately for their cause, they were not alone. In those days, having a complaint about the administration of land grants in New Mexico was hardly a mark of distinction. The entire territory was in a chaos of competing claims and doubtful titles.

It is therefore a matter worthy of respect, if not admiration, that in 1860, when the nation, riven by divisions over slavery and states' rights, was lurching toward civil war, Congress saw fit to select one New Mexico land grant from the scores in its backlog and to resolve its case with lavish generosity. Congress approved legislation, and President Buchanan signed it into law, whereby the Baca heirs might select land from the public domain of New Mexico Territory, which then included Arizona and southern Colorado, to replace *in full* the acreage of the original grant, from which their ancestors had failed to realize the least potential. That is to say, the government of the United States authorized a single family to select for their private use and benefit half a million acres in five separate tracts from the finest unoccupied land in the scarcely inventoried real estate cornucopia of the vast Southwest.

In the annals of wheedling wealth from the government, the achievement of New Mexico's Bacas stands as high as any. But it was not their achievement alone, or even mainly. For their first 100,000-acre tract the family selected the lush grazing lands of the Valles Caldera, already familiar to them, which lay upslope from the family home in Peña Blanca, near Cochiti. From at least the days of Cabeza de Baca onward, members of the family had herded livestock in the wild and dangerous commons of the valles, where raids by roving Navajos were a constant threat. With not so much as a nod in the direction of the Jemez or any other tribe that might have possessed an interest in it, the Bacas claimed a tract that surveyors mapped as a square roughly twelve miles on a side. The government awarded them title to the land, which was identified as Baca Location No. 1, and its boundaries set the basic outline for the eventual establishment of the Valles Caldera National Preserve. In acquiring the caldera, the family had obtained their primary goal, and they left the selection of Baca Locations 2 through 5 to their supremely effective lawyer, John S. Watts.

From the beginning, Watts had been the engineer and motive force behind the settlement of the Bacas' claim. As compensation for his services Watts assumed ownership of Locations 2, 3, and 4 (one each in what is now New Mexico, Arizona, and Colorado, respectively), and with fair dispatch he bought out the family's interest in No. 5 for less than a quarter of the amount for which he soon resold it. Watts completed his working life as a respected member of the New Mexico Supreme Court and in retirement returned to his home state of Indiana as a man of wealth and standing.

Matters did not proceed so smoothly for the Bacas. Ownership of the grant was initially divided among the eighteen living descendants of Cabeza de Baca and subsequently among their successive heirs. As years passed and ownership continued to fragment, members of the family sold their interests to outsiders, and control of the caldera gradually passed from the Bacas into the hands of real estate speculators. These worthies soon entwined the land and one another in a web of lawsuits, whose arguments they punctuated in 1883 with a shootout that left at least two men dead and one gravely wounded. This last, James G. Whitney, "a big, blustering fellow," later escaped his enemies by being lowered in the dark of night from a window of St. Vincent Hospital in Santa Fe.[1] The ultimate winner of this drawn-out fracas, who came away with undisputed ownership of the caldera in 1899, was Mariano S. Otero, a first cousin of one of the men who had been gunned down.

The ensuing decades witnessed a host of activities in and around the caldera. At various times road building, sulfur mining, homesteading, a hot springs resort, survey disputes, timber harvest, and the extensive use of the caldera for livestock grazing claimed the primary attention of Otero, his son Frederico, and the Redondo Development Company, a Pennsylvania investment company to which Frederico sold the Baca Location in 1909. But even as the engine of economic development coughed and sputtered, threatening to roar, there were others for whom the caldera's noneconomic attributes exerted a powerful attraction. Among these was Edgar L. Hewett, a perplexing and visionary impresario of multiple cultural causes, most of them dealing in one way or another with archaeology.

Hewett was the primary author of the American Antiquities Act of 1906, which conferred on the president authority to withdraw land from the public domain and establish national monuments in order to preserve sites of outstanding historical or scientific interest, including concentrations of archaeological ruins. Hewett also helped write the legislation creating the University of New Mexico and its sister institutions New Mexico State University and the New Mexico School of Mines (now the New Mexico Institute of Mining and Technology). A whirlwind of energy and more than a little bit megalomaniacal, he was the founding chairman of the Department of Anthropology at the University of New Mexico and the founding director of the Museum of New Mexico, the School of American Archaeology (later the School of American Research), and the San Diego Museum of Man, all of which posts he held simultaneously.

One of Hewett's abiding passions was the protection of the Southwest's archaeological heritage, and he was a key force behind the 1906 creation of Mesa Verde National Park, the nation's first preserve for cultural resources. Through the early decades of the 1900s, Hewett, the National Park Service, and others offered multiple, often competing visions for the creation of a national park on the Pajarito Plateau, which is the canyon and mesa country that separates the Valles Caldera from the Rio Grande. Formed from volcanic outflows of the caldera, the plateau harbored dozens of ancient villages, some of which clung spectacularly to the canyon sides—they were said to be the "cliff dwellings" of a "vanished" people, notwithstanding that the descendants of their original inhabitants lived a few miles away.

Undermined by discord between Hewett and his competitors, successive proposals for "Pajarito National Park" and "Cliff Cities National Park" succumbed to the combined resistance of private landowners, ranchers, Indian pueblos (the cliff and mesa ruins at Puye within the Santa Clara reservation were repeatedly targeted), and the young U.S. Forest Service, which had jurisdiction over much of the land the various parks would have embraced. The situation was somewhat defused in 1916 when President Woodrow Wilson proclaimed the establishment of Bandelier National Monument, but park advocates were not appeased. Bandelier, at 22,400 acres, was small, and until 1932 it remained under the management of the Forest Service. In 1923,

Hewett launched his grandest proposal. In alliance with the Park Service, he enlarged upon all previous park plans to include not just the Pajarito Plateau but all of the Baca Location as well. He and his allies sought to add scenic beauty and geologic drama to the "Cliff Cities National Park" in a way that would place it on a par with Mesa Verde or the Grand Canyon. With the support of the Santa Fe business community, they argued that such a park would stimulate the expansion of the region's embryonic tourist economy, while also assuring the preservation of a vital portion of the nation's patrimony. Hewett's and the Park Service's 1923 proposal was the first serious expression of federal interest in acquiring the Valles Caldera. Although the proposal failed for the same reasons as its predecessors, federal interest in the caldera would reassert itself with regularity over the decades to come.

Another Park Service proposal surfaced in 1938. This one—for creation of "Jemez Crater National Park"—was even more grandiose than Hewett's. It encompassed more than a million acres and emphasized the caldera's geological significance. It was vigorously opposed by the owner of the Baca, Frank Bond, an Española merchant and sheep grower, who had leased the grazing rights of the Baca since 1917 and who completed purchase of the property—all but its timber rights—from the Redondo Development Company in 1925.

Frank Bond died in 1945, and his son Franklin, who had managed the Baca since long before his father's death, passed away nine years later. In 1961, the Bond Estate Trust, which assumed ownership of the property, floated the idea of selling the Baca Location to the federal government. The trust's representatives contacted New Mexico's senior senator, Clinton P. Anderson, one of the Senate's most influential members, and, in his role as chairman of the Interior and Insular Affairs Committee, its leading arbiter on matters relating to public lands. Anderson took up the project with a passion and quickly

learned that both the Park Service and the Forest Service were fervent in their desire to acquire the land. But matters did not move forward rapidly. Anderson's conservative view of the value of the land was one obstacle. The agencies' jealousy and interference with each other was another. The Bond estate grew impatient. On January 1, 1963, it sold the property for $2.5 million to James Patrick Dunigan, an up-and-coming oilman from Abilene, Texas.

Dunigan started out with aggressive but vague plans for development of the property—he considered a racetrack, shops along the highway, possibly a golf course—but practical realities soon swept those ideas away. More important, the spell of the place began to capture him, as it had others. The spell, however, had no effect on the New Mexico Timber Company, which had acquired the Baca's logging rights from successors of the Redondo Development Company

and was cutting the ranch's old-growth timber at a determined and ever-increasing pace. Dunigan did not like what he saw. New Mexico Timber was snaking roads up the sides of mountain after mountain, taking every tree that would make a board. In 1964 Dunigan sued New Mexico Timber to alter its cutting practices, but the litigation had no immediate effect, except perhaps to speed the company's efforts to strip the Baca of its timber. Finally, in 1971, after the attrition of continuous legal action, Dunigan managed to buy back the timber rights to the property for $1.75 million, and the free-for-all clear-cutting and manic road building—in the end there were close to 1,500 miles of logging roads on the property—finally came to a halt.

As the 1970s drew to a close, Dunigan became convinced that the best and most appropriate future for the caldera lay in public ownership, and he offered the property to the National Park Service. But the director of the Park Service failed to appear for a crucial meeting, and, feeling rebuffed, Dunigan turned his attention to the U.S. Forest Service. Soon both agencies were eagerly pursuing acquisition. But once again, their mutual competition slowed progress, and suddenly, before a deal could be consummated, Dunigan succumbed to a fatal heart attack. Nearly twenty years would pass before his three sons were ready to pick up where he had left off.

BUYING THE BACA

Those twenty years, however, were not devoid of contact between the Dunigans and the government. In the 1960s James Patrick Dunigan had exchanged a small amount of land with the Forest Service, swapping a few hundred acres on the north boundary of the Baca for property of equal value adjacent to Santo Domingo Pueblo. In the 1980s, when a family company sought to lease the land for a cement plant, Santo Domingo sued to halt the project, claiming to be the parcel's rightful owner. Ultimately the Dunigans sold the property to the pueblo to settle the suit, but they did so at a considerable loss. People in the government noticed and were concerned, not least because they had been unable to honor the guarantees of good title the government had provided in the original land exchange.

Their concern was soon translated into legislation, enacted in 1990, that accomplished a number of goals. It permitted acquisition of two more small parcels from the Dunigans and provided the family compensation of $1.633 million. It also authorized—and this was the inspiration of a small group of professionals within the Department of Agriculture—a study of the Baca with special attention to the feasibility and desirability of its acquisition by the federal government. The report that resulted is rare among government documents. One of the forces behind it was Jim Snow, who was then deputy assistant general counsel in the department. According to Snow, "What we didn't want was a typical Forest Service report; what we wanted was something more like a real estate prospectus, something that would illustrate the Baca's public values and emphasize those values from a multiple-use perspective." Snow and his colleagues got what they wanted, and years later, the "Baca Report," freshly reprinted, would be an essential tool in an ultimately successful acquisition effort.

As the 1990s advanced, Snow stayed in touch with the family, and with Andrew Dunigan, one of the three sons, in particular. At one point, Andrew confided that he and his brothers were within a few years of being able to offer the property for sale. "When you do," said Snow, "we'd like first shot at it." "We'd like you to have it," came the reply.

First shot came in mid-1997, when Andrew, Mike, and Brian Dunigan called on New Mexico's senators and senior Agriculture and Forest Service staff for assistance. They were ready to explore a sale of the Baca Location No. 1 to the government. Would the senators sup-port such an effort? Senator Jeff Bingaman responded without hesitation. On September 24, 1997, he introduced a bill to authorize federal acquisition of the property and its inclusion in the National Forest System. This time, competition between the Forest Service and the Park Service, while still present, would not become the debilitating problem of the past. The agencies mutually acknowledged that the wishes of the Baca's sellers were clear and that its acquisition would be a Forest Service project. The Park Service, in Bingaman's bill, would not come away empty-handed. A portion of the headwaters of Bandelier National Monument that lay within the Baca would be transferred to the National Park System, as well as, potentially, certain Forest Service lands within the same watersheds. High officials within the Department of the Interior assured Bingaman that acquiring the land was of paramount importance; they would support the efforts of the Forest Service.

Meanwhile, New Mexico's other senator, Pete Domenici, the powerful chair of the Budget Committee, withheld his support. He said the federal government already owned too much of New Mexico and the rest of the West, and it should not attempt to buy more until it had fulfilled its existing acquisition commitments for national parks and other lands, which ran to hundreds of millions of dollars nationally. Nevertheless, he promised to study the matter and, implicitly, to gauge the level of public support the project generated.

The answer from that quarter was soon unequivocal, as Bingaman and other government officials made a succession of highly publicized visits to the caldera. The media took up the Baca's story, and publications from the *New York Times* to the *Santa Fe New Mexican* ran features with eye-catching photographs of mountain vistas and majestic elk. Public enthusiasm for the acquisition spread fast and ran deep. Two former secretaries of interior, Stewart Udall and Manuel Lujan, and three former directors of the New Mexico Game and Fish Department spoke out in favor of the acquisition. The Northern New Mexico Stockman's Association, recognizing that public use of the caldera's rangelands could ease regional grazing pressures, voiced its support. So did cities like Los Alamos and Santa Fe, as well as Sandoval and Rio Arriba counties, in which the property lay. A broad and vocal alliance of hunting, fishing, and environmental groups, along with veteran conservation leaders, organized themselves as the Baca Coalition specifically to drum up public support for the purchase, and the parent organizations of some of the coalition's members helped fan the flames of interest through their national magazines.

Still, the obstacles were daunting. The cost of the land would likely be as breathtaking as its scenery. When James Patrick Dunigan had discussed a sale to the government in 1980, the price he asked was reported to have approached $50 million. Now the owners hoped, and the frugal feared, it might run to twice that. A key to the outcome would be the position of the Clinton administration, which so far had not budgeted funds for the Baca in any of its proposals to Congress. The historical moment, however, looked promising. After decades of deficits, the government, boosted by a vigorous economy, was on a path to produce a budget surplus. It was likely that appropriations for land and water conservation would increase substantially in the coming fiscal years. On the negative side, however, was the general hostility of the Republican-controlled Congress to land acquisition, especially in the West, as well as its enmity toward the administration and its Democratic president.

In February 1998, President Clinton erased all doubt about his administration's position. On a visit to Los Alamos National Laboratory, Clinton addressed a large crowd at the main auditorium. He opened his remarks by saying, "Jeff Bingaman told me a good while ago, in no uncertain terms, that we had to move forward to protect the magnificent Valle Grande, 100,000 unspoiled acres near the Santa Fe forest [*sic*]. And in my budget, there is $40 million to support this project to secure this land."[2] The applause was loud and sustained.

In the spring of 1998, notwithstanding the nation's growing preoccupation with Monica Lewinsky and related scandals, it seemed that the planets were gradually aligning to favor federal purchase of the Baca. An appraisal undertaken by the Dunigan family was due by midsummer; the Forest Service realty staff would review it and, if possible, approve it for use as the basis for a purchase agreement; the $40 million promised by the president could serve as a down payment, with the balance to come in future years, if necessary. But still Domenici held out, and without his support, the project would not win congressional approval. At the time, New Mexico's powerful senior senator was unhappy with the Forest Service, particularly its handling of grazing issues in southern New Mexico. The thought of placing nearly 100,000 additional acres of the Southwest's choicest land under the agency's control was for him distinctly unappealing. Still less attractive was the possibility of making the Baca a national park, where grazing would have been excluded. So negatively did he consider these alternatives that for a brief period he considered assigning the property to the Bureau of Land Management, an action that would have illogically fragmented management of the Jemez Mountains, where the Baca was the "hole in the doughnut," surrounded almost entirely by Santa Fe National Forest. Although he gave no public encouragement to the project, Domenici and his staff continued to examine alternatives, wondering if the purchase of the Baca might be used as a means to address other long-standing issues besetting western public lands, including an abundance of litigation and appeals and the almost universal dissatisfaction among all parties with the results.

In July 1998 President Clinton made another trip to Albuquerque for a "town meeting" to discuss Social Security, in which Senator Domenici also participated. Following the meeting, at the president's invitation Senator Domenici joined Clinton on Air Force One for the flight back to Washington. Both men were prepared to discuss issues relating to nuclear nonproliferation and an upcoming legislative conference on the Energy and Water Appropriations Bill, which Domenici would chair. But the Baca was also on their mutual agenda.

The flight afforded Domenici a chance to present the fruits of his reflection about the proposed acquisition. He said he thought it was important to preserve the character of the Baca as a "working ranch of the highest environmental quality," and he suggested that, if the government acquired it, the property might be administered under an innovative trust structure similar to that which had recently been implemented for the Presidio in San Francisco. Domenici added that an agreement on the Baca should further include measures to address the disposition of surplus federal lands and to provide funds for prompt payment of "in-holders" whose lands federal agencies had identified for acquisition. Clinton said he had no serious objection to any of Domenici's points; he was eager to move ahead with the senator's plan as he had laid it out. The two men agreed to assign staff to an immediate drafting of a Statement of Principles capturing the elements of what they had discussed. All this took place on a Monday. By Friday the statement was ready, and the White House and Senator Domenici's office issued press releases to announce their agreement.

The Statement of Principles expressed the joint commitment of the White House and New Mexico's senators to draft and enact legislation authorizing federal acquisition of the Baca. Because "the unique nature of the Baca ranch requires a unique program for appropriate preservation, operation and maintenance," the legislation would establish a trust, whose directors the president would appoint, to carry out its program of protection and multiple use "including recreational opportunities, selective timbering, [and] limited grazing and hunting." The principles stipulated that management should "provide for the eventual financial self-sufficiency of the operation without violating other management goals," but they made clear that financial self-sufficiency should not be the sole test of the experiment's success or failure. Rather, the legislation to be drafted should "provide an opportunity for the Trust, should it not achieve financial self-sufficiency by its ninth year of operation, to continue operating upon agreement between Congress and the President, after showing rationale for not attaining a financially self-sufficient operation."[3] A second section of the Statement of Principles addressed the inventory and sale of surplus BLM lands and the use of the proceeds to fund purchase of inholdings in federal lands.

Supporters of the Baca acquisition greeted the news with both jubilation and perplexity. At last it seemed that the caldera would find its way into federal ownership and thus not become a trophy ranch for the superwealthy or, worse, be broken into smaller trophies, vacation cabins, and perhaps a resort. But the concept of the trust was an enigma, and many were suspicious. How would the board work? Who would run it? Would it be responsive to the public, or just to certain sectors?

The proposed Valles Caldera Preservation Act, rapidly drafted by aides of the two senators and by executive branch staff from the Department of Agriculture and the Council on Environmental Quality provided partial answers. On more than one occasion Domenici participated personally in the drafting sessions—a rare thing for a senator to do—and the result clearly bore his stamp. Where the original

Bingaman bill authorizing straightforward Forest Service acquisition of the Baca totaled three pages, the new one ran to twenty, fifteen of which dealt with the Valles Caldera. The bill specified that the land, once acquired, be designated the Valles Caldera National Preserve and that, although inventoried in the National Forest System, it was to be administered by a new entity, the Valles Caldera Trust, a federal corporation led by a nine-member board. The president, in consultation with the New Mexico congressional delegation, would appoint seven of those members, and they would represent diverse areas of expertise—forestry, ranching, wildlife management, financial management, local government, conservation, and the cultural and natural history of the region. The remaining two—the supervisor of Santa Fe National Forest and the superintendent of Bandelier National Monument—would serve ex officio, assuring coordination with the management of adjacent lands and bringing valuable federal experience to the deliberations of the board.

The purposes assigned to the trust were also diverse. It was to operate the preserve as a working ranch, while protecting and preserving the many values for which the land had been acquired—its scenery, fish and wildlife, history and culture, geology, recreational potential, and watershed function. It was to manage the renewable resources of the preserve for "multiple use and sustained yield." It was to provide for public recreation. And, "by optimizing income . . . without unreasonably diminishing the long-term scenic and natural values of the area," it was to achieve "a financially self-sustaining operation within 15 full fiscal years" (the earlier target of nine years having been lengthened).

The bill was introduced in both houses of Congress in October 1998, setting the stage for definitive federal action. The sole remaining mystery was how much the land would cost, but, strangely, delivery to the Forest Service of the Dunigans' appraisal of the Baca had been delayed.

Through the late summer and autumn of 1998, the Dunigans, along with Forest Service realty staff and lawyers for the Department of Agriculture, struggled to negotiate a confidentiality agreement specifying how information in the appraisal would be handled. The Dunigans sought a blanket prohibition against disclosure of any of the appraisal's contents. The government negotiators strove to comply, but, being constrained by law and the practicalities of the legislative process, they could not provide the ironclad guarantees the Dunigans desired. As one meeting yielded to the next and hard-earned agreements repeatedly broke down, communication grew increasingly strained. Finally, on January 7, 1999, the Dunigans abruptly faxed a letter to Janet Potts, counsel to the secretary of agriculture, announcing that they were withdrawing their offer to sell Baca Location No. 1 to the United States.

The reason, according to the public statement they soon issued, was the failure of the government to commit in writing to the promises of confidentiality its representatives had made earlier. The government had acted in bad faith, they implied, and the mutual trust necessary for serious negotiation was now unattainable.

Dismay was widespread. Domenici was "profoundly disappointed," Bingaman "deeply" so. Anger and incredulity were also much in evidence. "For something like this to fall apart on a confidentiality agreement is just bizarre," said Domenici's chief of staff, Steve Bell. "It just doesn't seem like enough . . . . We are very unhappy about it, and we have spent a lot of political capital on it."[4]

Speculation about the real reason for the Dunigans' withdrawal flourished. One theory held that a private buyer had offered them more money than the government was likely to pay. But that explanation begged the question of who might be spendthrift enough to outbid the government on so expensive a property. Another theory was counterintuitive: that perhaps the appraisal the Dunigans had commissioned had set too low a value for the property. If the appraisal's number was substantially lower than the owners expected and desired, they might have preferred to scuttle the deal rather than to have sold cheaply, or they might have wanted to get Congress to bypass the appraisal process altogether and set a price legislatively—a rare but not unheard-of strategy—in which case, concealing the appraisal's conclusions would be vital. Still another theory was that the Dunigans' appraisal was high enough to suit them, but they lacked confidence in it. If the appraisal was shaky in some respect and failed to meet federal standards, the Forest Service would likely refuse to approve it. The agency's rejection would become widely known, and this would undermine the family's ability to sell the ranch privately for top-of-the-market or above-market value. But all of this was conjecture, for no one in the government or outside Dunigan Enterprises ever saw the appraisal.

THE VALLES CALDERA NATIONAL PRESERVE

Newspaper columnists and others called for renewed talks. The *Santa Fe New Mexican* suggested that a new negotiating team representing the government, with no history of personal friction with the sellers, might do the trick. But no such strategy materialized; the talks were not rejoined, and within days, the Valles Caldera fell from the news. New Mexico and the rest of the nation had plenty of other things to think about, not least of which was the five-week Senate impeachment trial of President Clinton, which began on the same day the Dunigans announced the withdrawal of their offer to sell.

As in Edgar Hewett's day, and in Clinton Anderson's, and in the final years of James Patrick Dunigan's life, it seemed that the acquisition of the Baca Location by and for the American people was not meant to be. The tide of opportunity seemed to have passed. As the winter of 1999 gave way to spring and spring to summer, there was no news about the splendid ranch in the vast caldera at the top of the Jemez Mountains. Steers were delivered in May and grazed the valles as usual. Every day or so, a logging truck turned in through the main gate and later came out loaded. The rhythms of the ranch, centered on livestock and a modest amount of logging, plus elk hunts, which got under way as September began, continued as in previous years.

And so the announcement on September 8, 1999, that a deal had been struck caught New Mexico and the interested world by surprise. It came as a joint announcement by Andrew Dunigan, CEO of the Baca Land and Cattle Company, and George Frampton, acting chairman of the White House Council on Environmental Quality. Subject to the necessary appropriations by Congress, the Dunigans would sell the Baca to the U.S. government for $101 million.

Andrew Dunigan explained to the press that "After the dust settled, tensions were reduced," and the general level of communication improved. And so informal talks resumed, leading to the agreement. What he said was unquestionably true, but he left even more unsaid. Had the Dunigans approached a select list of potential buyers and found no one with motivation as strong and pockets as deep as the government's? No one outside the family knew for sure. One factor behind the sudden improvement of communication, however, was clear: the Dunigans had obtained a new appraisal by a new appraiser. This one came in at $101 million. The Dunigans submitted it to the same Forest Service realty team they had worked with before.[5] Measures for ensuring confidentiality, in this instance, were strict but still fell under standard rules and procedures. The Forest Service reviewed

the appraisal with alacrity and communicated its approval to the Dunigans. Then followed the hurried but painstaking negotiation of an exchange of letters. In one the Forest Service confirmed its approval of the appraisal and offered to buy the Baca for $101 million. In the other, the Dunigans' New Mexico attorney expressed his clients' intent to sell the property to the government at the appraised value, subject to the timely appropriation of funds. The letters were signed and exchanged on September 7, 1999, a Tuesday. On Wednesday the 8th, Andrew Dunigan and George Frampton made their announcement.

The fate of the Baca now lay with Congress. Domenici and Bingaman reintroduced the Valles Caldera Preservation Act, with slight alterations. Most of the changes provided clarification or addressed procedural issues that had not previously been anticipated. But one was substantive. It authorized the government to assign a portion of its rights to acquire the Baca to Santa Clara Pueblo. This provision had resulted from a negotiation almost as long and nearly as contentious as that which concerned the primary purchase.

The rim of the caldera is a circle. The boundaries of the Baca Location form a square overlapping it. Lands in the southeast corner lying outside the caldera would be assigned to Bandelier National Monument. The new provision in the bill would allow similar lands in the northeast corner to be bought by Santa Clara. These were the headwaters of Santa Clara Creek, the lifeline of the pueblo.

The headwaters had been excluded from the original Pueblo League—the land grant, formed in a square, two leagues on a side, that the Spanish colonial government conveyed to the Santa Clara tribe in 1689. Subsequent creation of the Baca Location effectively, if unjustly, confirmed this exclusion and seemed to foreclose the possibility of reuniting the headwaters with the rest of Santa Clara's reservation. But for three centuries, Santa Clara refused to relinquish its claim, and when the Dunigans initially offered the property for sale to the U.S. in 1997, Santa Clara's representatives clamored to participate in the negotiations. They claimed that the headwaters, as well as additional lands, belonged to them as a matter of right and law, and in the course of arguing their cause they discovered a new and powerful ally—the Lannan Foundation of Santa Fe, which ultimately agreed to buy on their behalf their share of Baca lands.

The rightness of reuniting the headwaters with the pueblo was never seriously in dispute. The question was how to accomplish it—if indeed it could be accomplished at all. An outright gift of land from the government to the pueblo was not possible, barring special legislation, and the federal negotiators viewed special legislation as anathema because of the precedent it would set. Moreover, they were loath to entertain strategies that might upset their delicate relations with the Dunigans. They also vigorously resisted Santa Clara's efforts to acquire lands outside the topographic watershed of Santa Clara Creek. But Santa Clara's representatives were nothing if not persistent, and eventually, after a great deal of strain and effort, a simple and elegant solution emerged: the government would assign to Santa Clara rights to acquire the headwaters directly from the Dunigans; Santa Clara, through its patron the Lannan Foundation, would pay a price consistent with what the government was paying, thus ensuring that the Dunigans received the full amount they were due. Santa Clara and the government would also exchange conservation easements preserving the integrity of the lands along their future common boundary. Because all of this would be accomplished without the federal government entering the chain of title for the headwaters land, no difficult legal precedents would be triggered or set.

The planned transaction constituted a rare and gratifying opportunity to correct a long-standing historical injustice, and if the bill passed and the necessary, gigantic appropriation was made, the remedy would occur. But those were very big ifs. In the fractious 106th Congress, with the Democratic White House and the Republican leadership on Capitol Hill continually at odds, the highest priorities of the people's business suffered long delays, and items that were optional, local, and expensive, like the acquisition of the Baca, were exceptionally difficult to accomplish.

To make matters worse, the acquisition had enemies. Some of the conservative Republican members of the Senate vehemently opposed any enlargement of the federal estate, never mind a $101 million and nearly 100,000-acre ranch in a state already dominated by federal land. But it was dangerous for them to directly attack a project championed by the powerful chair of the Budget Committee. A safer tactic was to request a review of the Baca appraisal by the General Accounting Office (since renamed the Government Accountability Office, but more commonly known as the GAO). If the GAO found fault with the valuation, the project might be weakened enough to kill.

Indeed the GAO did find fault. The appraisal was too high by half, it said, instantly dimming prospects for both the Baca authorization bill and the appropriation. The press took up the argument, and newspapers in Albuquerque and Santa Fe gave prominent play to opinions pro and con. The GAO's arguments had to be defeated, and so Domenici and Bingaman sought a showdown. At their request, the Senate Subcommittee on Forests and Public Lands Management scheduled a hearing on Senate Bill 1892, the Valles Caldera Preservation Act, for March 10, 2000.

The hearing provided a thorough public airing for the bill that both authorized purchase of the land and created the Valles Caldera Trust to manage it. Most critically it afforded a forum for the GAO, the Forest Service, and the Dunigans' appraiser, Laurie Van Court, to present their arguments and for the senators to question them. When the appraisal discussion was complete, it was clear that the defense of the Van Court appraisal by the Forest Service and the Dunigans had prevailed—and another obstacle was overcome.

At the hearing Bingaman and Domenici made statements about the bill they had cosponsored, and Domenici, as architect of the Valles Caldera Trust, used the occasion to underscore his view that the trust's attainment of financial self-sufficiency was a goal, one of several, that the trust would pursue. It was something the trust should strive to accomplish, but it was not the be-all and end-all of the experiment, as some of the bill's critics had been arguing in the press.

Witnesses came and went. The undersecretary for Natural Resources and the Environment in the Department of Agriculture testified, as did officials of the Forest Service and the Bureau of Land Management (who addressed issues in Title II of the bill concerning land disposal). A delegation from Jemez Pueblo pleaded that two hundred acres at the top of Redondo Peak should be awarded to them so that their holy sites might be protected, as Santa Clara's would be. The owner of a minority share of mineral interests underlying the caldera asked for a speedy buyout, even if it required condemnation—but at a price far higher than the value placed on minerals in the Dunigans' appraisal. And the parade of witnesses continued, each expressing support for the bill.

The hearing also drew written testimony from a number of people who had been invited to appear in person but were unable to make the trip to Washington, including me. I had been on the edges of the project from early on, visiting the property late in 1997 with administration officials, discussing it with the Dunigans in a limited

fashion on a couple of occasions, and participating in the environmental coalition organized to support the purchase. Having worked on similar although much smaller land conservation projects, I was acquainted with most of the congressional figures and Forest Service staff involved with the Baca.

What I said in my written testimony was essentially a repetition of the combined support and concern I had expressed to the authors of the Valles Caldera Preservation Act from the time of their earliest drafts: that the Baca was a national treasure; that its federal acquisition would unify management of the Jemez Mountains; that Santa Clara's acquisition of the Santa Clara Creek headwaters was good for all parties; and that creation of the Valles Caldera Trust was a worthwhile and legitimate experiment in federal land management.

My concerns were specific. Most serious was the ambiguity of the purposes of the Valles Caldera Trust. The legislation instructed the trust to develop a management program directed toward six goals:

1. Operation of the preserve as a working ranch
2. Protection and preservation of the preserve's salient qualities
3. Multiple use and sustained yield of renewable resources
4. Public use and access for recreation
5. Use of renewable resources to benefit local communities, enhance management coordination with adjacent federal entities, and achieve economic efficiencies
6. Optimization of income

I worried that the six goals were—or at least had the potential to be—mutually contradictory, and that it was essential to prioritize among them, lest the board of the trust be perpetually uncertain or divided on how to interpret their instructions from Congress. I urged that the second goal be identified as primary and the others be subject to the limits it imposed.

I also urged that the relation of the management goals to the goal of financial self-sufficiency, which was set forth separately in the bill, be clarified. With too much emphasis on profit making, such non-economic activities as scientific monitoring, fire management, public involvement, and other matters vital to successful management of the preserve might be neglected. Moreover, unless the bill gave a clearer idea of how "management success" should be measured, many observers would evaluate the trust strictly in terms of its pursuit of economic self-sufficiency. Worse, the board of the trust might take a similarly narrow view. I urged—in vain, as it turned out—that the bill emphasize that the trust would be evaluated in terms of its success in pursuing all of the goals with which it was charged and in terms of the public confidence and support it earned in pursuing them.

The hearing resulted in a number of mostly technical changes in the bill, but one change was substantive. In the markup that followed, language was added to prohibit ground-disturbing activities and motorized access (except for essential administrative purposes) on Redondo Peak above 10,000 feet in elevation. Jemez Pueblo would not received title to the mountaintop, as it had requested, but the legislation would provide their sacred sites an additional layer of protection.

The Senate Committee on Energy and Natural Resources sent the bill, as amended, to the full Senate on April 12, 2000. The Senate passed it by unanimous consent the following day. House action took longer, but an identical bill, shepherded by New Mexico representatives Heather Wilson and Tom Udall, passed the full House on July 12, 2000, by a vote of 377 to 45. The enormous $101 million appropria-tion having already been approved,[6] only the president's signature was lacking. A signing ceremony was set for July 25. It was to take place in the Roosevelt Room of the White House, and several dozen people who had been involved in the acquisition would be present, including the Dunigan brothers, senators Bingaman and Domenici, representatives Wilson and Udall, the governor of Santa Clara Pueblo, the secretary of the Department of Agriculture, and the chairman of the Council on Environmental Quality. All the necessary deeds and other documents had been executed and placed in escrow pending the president's signature so that, as soon as the president made the enacted bill law, the greater part of the Baca Location No. 1, with a few additional signatures, would become the property of the United States.

But there was a hitch in the plan for pomp and circumstance, small for the Baca, big for the world. President Clinton was hosting peace negotiations between Israel and the Palestinian Authority at Camp David. A resolution of the Middle East conflict had never been so close, but on July 24, the discussions broke down. Clinton stayed at Camp David in an attempt to achieve a last-ditch compromise, and he signed the Baca bill there. On July 25, as Clinton announced that the collapse of the peace talks was irreparable, the now anticlimactic reception in the Roosevelt Room took place without him. Meanwhile, the transfer of federal funds to the Dunigans was initiated. Normally such a transfer, which required a labyrinthine series of bureaucratic reviews and approvals, would have taken weeks. In this instance, because of whip-cracking at the highest levels, it was accomplished in hours. As a result, by nightfall on July 25, 2000, and after transfer of 823 acres to Bandelier and the purchase of 5,045 acres by Santa Clara, the Baca Location No. 1 had become the 88,900-acre Valles Caldera National Preserve, and it belonged to the American people.

GETTING STARTED

The federal acquisition of the Baca was an extraordinary achievement. It required willing sellers, tireless and top-flight agency work, bipartisan political commitment, and a colossal sum of money. Perhaps $101 million is not a large amount compared to the purchase of attack aircraft or the operation of a naval squadron, but relative to normal government expenditures for conservation lands, it is extreme. It exceeds the amount the Forest Service had paid for any other single acquisition in its long history. In theory, the Land and Water Conservation Fund, from which the revenue for the Baca purchase was drawn, receives hundreds of millions of dollars each year from a dedicated source—the offshore oil and gas leases of the nation—but the idea that these funds are functionally separate from the rest of the federal budget is a fiction. In order for such a large appropriation to have been made for the benefit of so small a state as New Mexico, two conditions had to be met. First, New Mexico had to have political clout far out of proportion to its small population, and this the state had in the person of Senator Pete Domenici, a Republican then in his fifth term in the Republican-controlled Senate and beyond question one of the most powerful New Mexican delegates to Congress in the history of the state. Second, there had to be the perception that the nation could afford large gifts to itself, and briefly in the last years of the Clinton administration, this also was the case—so much so that in the presidential campaign of 2000, the question of what to do with the newly achieved budget surplus became a hotly debated issue (albeit soon erased by tax cuts and war). Added to these vital assets was the personal commitment of President Clinton, which elevated purchase of the Baca to the status of a first-rank national priority and empowered key members of his administration to expedite matters that might otherwise have ensnarled the project in delay and red tape.

Taken together, all of these favorable conditions make clear that the completion of the project depended upon an alignment of political planets that is seldom achieved.

Now that the hard work of acquisition was complete, other hard work had to begin. The first order of business was the selection of a board of trustees for the new Valles Caldera Trust. No application process existed, but letters of interest from prospective candidates soon rained on the New Mexico congressional delegation and the Council on Environmental Quality (CEQ). With the encouragement of friends both inside and outside the government, I contributed my own to the downpour.

Then came a long wait. The CEQ, working with the delegation, decided on a slate of nominees in early autumn of 2000. The White House reviewed and approved it. The FBI conducted background checks. By the time the names could be made public, it was December. My name was among them. Our notification was a faxed copy of a White House press release—not exactly a letter of appointment, but it would have to do. The new board would meet for a couple of days of orientation at a hotel in Santa Fe during the second week of January 2001, even as the stalwarts of the Clinton administration were packing up their desks and preparing to vacate their offices prior to the inauguration of George W. Bush ten days later. After that, we would pretty much be on our own.

The orientation consisted of a series of presentations on government procedures, ethics, and the responsibilities we were about to assume. A procession of specialists from the Forest Service and other agencies briefed us on the character of the caldera and the condition of its various "resources"—to the extent that the condition was known. Janet Potts, counsel to the secretary of agriculture, swore us in. She also presented each of us with a thick binder notebook her staff had prepared covering topics as disparate as legislative intent and travel vouchers. It was all the help that, under the circumstances, anyone could give us.

Bob Armstrong, who had served as assistant secretary for lands and minerals in the Department of the Interior in the first Clinton administration and who for many years sat on the Texas Parks and Wildlife Commission, occupied the wildlife seat. Karen Durkovich, a former chair of the New Mexico chapter of the Nature Conservancy, was the conservation representative. Palemon Martinez, the secretary-treasurer of the Northern New Mexico Stockman's Association, held the grazing position. Former state senator Steve Stoddard, who had long been active in economic development and banking in Los Alamos, assumed the business and finance position. Tom Swetnam, a forest ecologist and head of the Laboratory of Tree-Ring Research at the University of Arizona, was the board's forest expert. David Yepa, a member of Jemez Pueblo and its general counsel, filled the slot for local government. I was the cultural and natural historian. Leonard Atencio, who in the previous year had contended with the devastating Cerro Grande fire (which burned whole mountainsides immediately east of the Baca and consumed homes in Los Alamos), joined the board by virtue of his position as supervisor of the Santa Fe National Forest. Dennis Vasquez, the young new superintendent of Bandelier National Monument, represented the National Park Service.

It was a diverse, experienced, talented, and bipartisan group. I felt honored to be part of it, and still more so when they elected me chairman. I agreed to serve for a trial period of three months, after which the board would have the option of making a change. (As circumstance would have it, I served as chair until the expiration of my appointment in January 2005.)

Toward the close of the orientation session, we assessed our position. We needed a staff, a budget, a work plan, and bylaws. We owned not so much as a file cabinet or a telephone. We had no office. Our instructions consisted of fifteen pages of federal legislation, Potts's notebook, and a labyrinth of federal rules, regulations, and procedures that no single individual could master. Our operational funding for the next nine months—the remainder of fiscal year 2001—was set at a barely custodial level and would not sustain our initiating anything substantial. Our most important friends in the executive branch, those who knew and cared about the Valles Caldera, from the president down through the leadership of the CEQ and the secretariat of the Department of Agriculture, even to the scheduling secretary in the Office of the Chief of the Forest Service, were leaving the government or changing jobs, and their replacements in some cases would not be named or confirmed for months and would be preoccupied with learning their jobs and tending to emergencies for more months after that.

The preserve itself was snowbound and inaccessible and would remain so until May. It had no equipment and no furnishings. In vacating the ranch, the Dunigans had carted off every hammer and bucket, drinking glass and bed, even to the point of removing the weather vane from the roof of the hunting lodge.

We knew better what the preserve did not have than what it did, for we entirely lacked the kind of baseline ecological information that was a prerequisite for legally and publicly acceptable land-use programs. We also lacked any form of agreement with the Game and Fish Department on hunting, fishing, or wildlife management and with the Historic Preservation office concerning the archaeological clearance that had to precede all varieties of ground disturbance, including the grading and repair of existing ranch roads. We needed to introduce ourselves to our neighbors: the agencies we would be working with, the administrations of the three counties (Sandoval, Rio Arriba, and Los Alamos) that included or bordered the preserve, and the neighboring pueblos that possessed strong religious and cultural ties to the caldera. Expectations were high. We especially needed to reach out and connect with the general public, which understandably wanted to know what we proposed to do. And the board itself needed to cohere, to get comfortable working with one another, and, not least, to learn how to handle our disagreements. We had plenty to do.

Early on, we were obliged to play a fair amount of defense: a few members of the Game Commission seemed to regard the Valles Caldera Trust as an upstart that needed to be taught its place. In February we informed the commission that we would not be ready for an elk hunt the following fall—arrangements for the lottery we contemplated would take time to develop, but the commission's annual regulations needed to be published immediately—and so we asked that the caldera be closed to hunting for 2001. Unfortunately, the commission did not look kindly on our request. A week later, I rushed to a Game Commission meeting to address their suddenly announced plans to schedule a hunt in spite of our objection. My reception was decidedly hostile, but after members of the commission vented copious amounts of steam, the motion to schedule a major hunt for the caldera was defeated by one vote.

In March Swetnam and I went to Washington to plead for more funds from the Forest Service for the upcoming summer field season. Without supplemental funds and the work those funds would make possible, we would have little to show for our first year of operation. We especially needed funds to initiate the baseline inventory and ecological monitoring that would enable us to evaluate the likely impacts of future programs. The Forest Service administrators received us sym-

pathetically but expressed doubt about making a budget adjustment in time to help us. Then, only a month later, one of their top managers called to say she was transferring $350,000 to us—nearly our entire request. We were overjoyed. We waited for the money to arrive. And waited. A sign-off from the secretary of agriculture was lacking here. A go-ahead from the Office of Management and Budget was needed there. Deadlines for contracting summer work slipped by. It was deep in summer when we learned that the House and Senate Appropriations Committees would have to approve the reprogramming of funds, and it was August when we learned that the approvals would not be forthcoming. Our education in the workings of Washington was proceeding apace.

Budgetary challenges, including efforts to secure funding for fiscal year 2002, continued through the year. (The new Bush administration took little interest in the Valles Caldera, regarding the public lands experiment as a pet project of Senator Domenici—in budgetary terms an "earmark," and no concern of theirs.) We also labored hard to recruit first interim, then permanent staff, and the more we struggled with Washington, the more we realized we needed someone with Capitol Hill experience to lead our organization, even more than we needed a land manager. We realized with ever-greater clarity that we faced two major tasks. One was to develop the Valles Caldera Trust as a functioning institution, capable of protecting and administering the public use of one of the premier landscapes in the American West. The other was to develop the infrastructure and programs that would shape that use. The first task was out of the public view, entangled in red tape, and involved little that anyone outside the organization would cheer about. But it had to progress in order for us to make headway on the second task, which had the potential for drama and impact. The programs were what everybody was waiting for.

and around the Jemez Mountains. Each had its own character and was a kind of revelation. Attending them was like taking a postgraduate course in the diversity and complexity of northern New Mexico. In Jemez Springs, the people who made comments spoke as much to one another as to the board, and when they said how much they wanted to get into the preserve and enjoy it, they made clear that other people with different interests should be accommodated, too. Santa Fe was almost the reverse. Few of the speakers acknowledged the presence of the others in the room, but each had strong feelings and spoke as though he or she held a franchise on correct answers. At Ghost Ranch, near Abiquiu, the modest turnout consisted entirely of ranchers, and grazing was the only subject that elicited interest. In Los Alamos, a city of scientists and engineers, more than two hundred people filled the meeting hall. Many were organized into volunteer groups and study committees, each of which had a designated spokesperson. The meeting lasted long into the night, and nearly every presenter provided the board with written comments in multiple copies.

Some of the suggestions came from far afield. One proposal asked that we dedicate the Valle Grande as a meeting place for the elders of the world, where, in collective council, the globe's severest problems might be solved. The proponents assured us that Nelson Mandela and the Dalai Lama would participate. Another proposal, taking to heart our charge to operate as a "working ranch," urged that we go one better and develop the preserve as a nineteenth-century working ranch, the kind of place where the Virginian, Hoss Cartwright, and the boys from *Lonesome Dove* would feel at home. It would be a Williamsburg of the golden decades of the American West, replete with appropriately costumed staff. The proponents were untroubled that the Baca had never been a nineteenth-century cattle ranch, nor that the golden

In the public arena, our first order of business was to listen. Before the board began discussing specific programs and before its members began to identify themselves with specific positions, we needed to hear what people who cared about the caldera had to say. We organized a series of seven listening sessions in communities in

West, looked at closely, is more paint than gilding. But these kinds of suggestions were exceptions. Most of what we heard was thoughtful and considerate of both the land and the people who are drawn to it.

As the listening tour drew to a close, the board held a retreat at Bandelier National Monument. (It was late April 2001, but we still couldn't get into the preserve. After a winter of heavy snowfall, the East Fork of the Rio Jemez was so swollen with snowmelt that it was running *over* the main bridge on the entrance road.) We reviewed the comments we'd received and tried to identify the common threads. The central message seemed to be this: "The place we've known as the Baca is fine as it is. Don't screw it up. We've been looking at it over the fence for years, and we want to get in there and get to know and use it, each in our fashion, but we know that, if we all go in at once, we'll love the place to death. So go slow. Open it gradually. Limit the amount of each kind of use. We are willing to wait our turn."

At the Bandelier retreat, the board drafted a set of management principles in which we tried to join the essence of what we'd heard from the public with the core of our instructions from Congress. The principles stressed fiscal restraint, protection of the preserve's heritage and essential character, and development of programs that would emphasize quality over the quantity of experiences the preserve would provide. We discussed at length—and by no means for the last time— the triple bind in which we found ourselves: that the clearest path to financial self-sufficiency depended on developing programs with low costs and high returns; that high returns meant charging high fees to a few people or moderate fees to many, and that in either case, the cost of experiencing the caldera might exceed what people of modest means or families with children could afford; and that assuring a high level of environmental quality in our stewardship of the land, as well as management excellence in vital areas that produced no income—such

as public communication, pueblo relations, and environmental and archaeological compliance—required substantial staff time and was inherently expensive.

These tensions ran to the heart of the Valles Caldera experiment. Early on, we resolved that we would commit ourselves to an ethic of social equity—that although we might develop elite, expensive programs for a small number of wealthy participants, we would assure that people from all socioeconomic strata would be able to access every major activity on the preserve, at some level and in some way. This commitment seemed to us an essential part of the American social contract: that all citizens, regardless of economic station, should have access to the nation's public lands. Some critics of the Valles Caldera experiment, focusing on the financial self-sufficiency language in the Valles Caldera Preservation Act, had characterized it as a "privatization of a public asset," and we were determined to prove them wrong. We were in close contact with the authors of the legislation—one of them, Gary Ziehe, was the trust's first executive director—and they assured us that financial self-sufficiency was "a goal, not a mandate," and that it should not trump the other goals the trust was instructed to pursue. The committee report for the Valles Caldera Preservation Act (essentially a documentation of Congress's legislative intent) affirmed this view:

> The Committee expects that economic self-sufficiency is a goal of the Trust, and while optimizing the generation of income, it shall not interfere with good management principles or unreasonably diminish scenic and natural values of the area. The Trust should generate revenue while considering local needs. Reasonable and customary grazing fees, grass banking, and hunting fees are among the options the Trust may pursue within its management program.[7]

It was clear that Congress had given us abundant flexibility, along with fifteen years, to build our businesses and prove our financial mettle. Nevertheless, the question of how to turn a profit loomed large, even as we set about the many tasks that awaited us. Among the most pressing were building a staff, organizing an office, securing funding, repairing infrastructure, inventorying resources, fending off geothermal drilling projects, and developing policies and procedures for a seemingly limitless list of necessary administrative functions (environmental analysis, law enforcement cooperation, religious access, purchasing, personnel, and on and on). And of course we needed to build programs for hunting, grazing, and various kinds of recreation. We needed to generate revenue from those programs, and we needed to do so in a way that elicited public support for the preserve. Our instructions from Congress made clear that the Valles Caldera Trust was a combined experiment in both land management and economics. No one needed to add that it was also a political experiment. We fully understood that if we alienated the constituencies whose support had made possible the creation of the preserve, the enterprise as a whole would fail.

ECONOMICS

To be sure, there are ways to achieve high returns from programs without charging high prices and obtaining wide margins. A supermarket makes money on narrow margins by selling to a high volume of customers. But the Valles Caldera could not be a natural-resource supermarket. The wear and tear of too much commodity production or recreational traffic would ruin the place, much as it has compromised many national forests and parks. A lottery is another way to build revenue from a large customer base, but with the added virtue, from the operator's point of view, of limiting the obligation to distribute "product." We used lotteries to good effect with our early elk hunts. The cost of entry was low—twenty dollars a chance—and we generated substantial returns by attracting thousands of entrants. Losers did not lose much and winners won a great deal. In 2002, our first year of elk hunting, we grossed just under $500,000 and netted almost $200,000. We thought, "This is a business we can grow successfully." Even so, the most profitable part of the program depended on the handful of elk hunting opportunities we auctioned to high-dollar hunters for upward of $10,000 a hunt, which was a kind of echo of the elite hunting program the Dunigans had run.

The economics of the elk program collapsed, however, when the New Mexico Game Commission, backed by a 2004 attorney general's opinion, reversed its previous position and ruled that hunting in the Valles Caldera was subject to a limitation imposed elsewhere in New Mexico that reserved 78 percent of elk licenses on public-land hunting for state residents. The legal reasoning behind the ruling was logical, if debatable (the trust argued that its organic legislation conferred an exemption), but it destroyed the trust's ability to market the elk lottery nationally. At the same time, the commission withdrew its permission for the trust to auction a small number of hunting opportunities to the highest bidder. To no one's surprise, hunting revenue plummeted in 2004, and the program barely broke even. (Resolving this impasse will likely require legislative action at the state or federal level.)

Grazing produced worse results, but for reasons that were sometimes surprising. The federal government does not buy insurance; it self-insures. But because the Valles Caldera Trust is not closely supervised by line officers of the executive branch, it is excluded from access to the federal Judgment Fund and must seek insurance in the private market. This proved exceedingly expensive when we sought workmen's compensation insurance for our cowboys, who admittedly practice a risky occupation. Obtaining such coverage was imperative, for economic as well as moral reasons: besides ruining a life, one broken back from a horse wreck could have bankrupted the trust. To make a long story short, the insurance issue, exacerbated by federal rules on overtime and other technical considerations, drove the labor costs of our early, small-scale grazing program to unsustainable levels.

In drafting the Valles Caldera Preservation Act, the bill's authors had presumed, quite reasonably, that since the Dunigans had operated the Baca as a profitable working ranch, the Valles Caldera Trust ought to be able to do the same. But the truth of the matter proved more complex. What the trust learned in its early years—and what it continues to wrestle with—is that a federal corporation, even one as autonomous as the trust, is a different species of organization from a private ranch. It is subject to a host of laws, rules, and regulations, some of which, like the National Environmental Policy Act, are well known, while others, like restrictions that limit the trust to a short list of expensive institutional account managers and bookkeepers, are essentially invisible to outside observers. Compliance with such laws and regulations is expensive. In addition, a federal entity is—and should be—held to higher standards of performance than a private enterprise. Although the Dunigans' land management practices were generally well conceived and well executed, especially in the later years of their tenure, and although the lands of the caldera were on the whole improving in ecological health and resilience under their care, neither their grazing program nor their timber operation would have escaped protests and legal action had they been the work of a federal entity.

As our efforts progressed, a number of us involved with the Valles Caldera Trust became convinced that analyzing the cost differential between the operation of a federal corporation and a private

entity would provide useful information. We thought of the difference as "federal overhead." Besides the items already mentioned, such a category might include the cost of archaeological survey and mitigation, ecological monitoring, public involvement in decision making, pueblo relations, and certain essential educational responsibilities, as well as other functions.

Optimists have claimed that if profits from revenue-producing areas fail to cover these overhead items, then a well-crafted private fund-raising program might make up the difference. I may be too jaded in my view, but, having devoted a fair portion of my professional life to fund-raising, I doubt very much that private philanthropy can be enticed to cover such core operational responsibilities. Philanthropy can play a large role at the preserve in launching new initiatives and funding special programs, but the costs that collectively constitute "federal overhead" are unlikely candidates for sustained grant making.

Placing aside the funding of overhead for a moment, I believe that in the long term the major activities of the preserve, consistent with the goals of the Valles Caldera Preservation Act, can be financially self-sustaining, but I have a lasting concern. To return to the language of the committee report (and similar language in the act), it is clear that economic gains should not be won at the cost of "unreasonable" diminishment of scenic and natural values, but just what would "reasonable" diminishment be and how might future boards interpret so vague an idea? The term "unreasonable" was inserted in the act in order to preempt objections to minor and small-scale alterations of the landscape, such as the temporary construction of a movie set. Nevertheless, it is difficult to imagine any permanent or unqualified diminishment that would be reasonable in so splendid a place.

In addition, even if hunting, fishing, grazing, hiking, and other activities become self-funding, they are unlikely to generate sufficient collective profit to fully offset the preserve's federal overhead, and I strongly believe that the preserve's resources should not be squeezed hard or dedicated to an exclusively wealthy clientele in an attempt to do so. Congress should defray all or most of the cost of federal overhead. It should fulfill its part of the social contract. Our federal budget brims with optional expenditures. Tending to the people's business at the Valles Caldera should not be considered optional.

PLANS AND PROGRAMS

Neglected in this essay thus far is any discussion of recreation, just as recreation was neglected in the first years of the trust's operations. The first neglect is of no importance; the second, however, touches issues that underscore the challenges faced by the Valles Caldera Trust.

We were slow in opening hiking trails because each trail required archaeological clearance, which took time. Surveys could only be conducted when the ground was free of snow, after which the necessary report writing and review process commandeered their own little portions of eternity, leading finally, if all went well, to clearance. A more serious issue was transportation: how to delivers hikers to the desired trailhead, or anglers to the appointed fishing beat. Early in its discussions, the board agreed that allowing significant numbers of private vehicles on the back roads of the caldera was a bad idea. The roads of the preserve are rough, like ranch roads everywhere, and they can be especially treacherous in foul weather. We knew of no fair way to discriminate between visitors who possessed the experience and vehicles our roads demanded and those who were likely to break down or get lost or stuck. We worried too about the effect of people and traffic on wildlife and about the inevitable safety and rescue issues that would arise when two vehicles in a hurry tried to share a blind curve from opposite directions. Even more we reflected on the predicament of the West's most popular national parks, places like Yosemite and the south rim of the Grand Canyon, where the scenery wears a veil of automobile exhaust and the visitor experience is defined first by traffic congestion and scarce parking spaces and only after that by the splendor of the land. The leading exception outside of Alaska was Zion National Park, which has excluded cars in favor of a carefully designed bus system that pleases visitors, local businesses, and park officials equally.

We knew that as much as the preserve needed anything, it needed a comprehensive transportation plan (which might or might not ultimately be the basis for a system like Zion's). And we knew that deciding the future of transportation within the preserve would effectively decide the character of the preserve, for the way that people moved through the place would affect everything: the infrastructure, the quality of visitor experiences, the shape and function of programs. We also knew that developing such a plan would require the expertise of the best professionals in the nation as well as the focused energy of the trust's board and staff. Until we had it in place, we'd keep experimenting with small-scale visitor programs and learn what we could. Unfortunately, this course left us dependent on multi-passenger vans that the General Service Administration provided, which were designed for highways and cities, not roads like ours. The vans ferrying people around the preserve deteriorated fast, and riding in them was not a pleasure. We were impatient to commence transportation planning and knew it would be a giant undertaking. We thought we were approaching readiness to launch it, but first we had yet another plan to complete.

The Valles Caldera Preservation Act instructed the trust to prepare "a comprehensive program for the management of land, resources, and facilities within the Preserve," giving us two years from the date we assumed management responsibility from the secretary of agriculture to complete it. (This delegation, long delayed by financial difficulties, was finally made August 2, 2002.) As we embarked on this task we soon realized that we lacked essential information about the preserve and the possibilities of its programs. No other organization was quite like ours, and no one else had much experience doing what we were setting out to do. Without a good deal of experimentation and testing, we could do little but make big guesses about the future. Moreover, if our plan was going to achieve the level of specificity that the legislation and the general public seemed to expect, we would necessarily have to make a host of concrete decisions about how the preserve would operate, and this "decisional" character would require that our plan become a full-blown environmental impact statement, further raising the need for quality information rather than guesswork. We judged, without the least doubt, that completing a defensible environmental impact statement within the time available was impossible.

Instead we elected to strive for comprehensiveness, but to stop just short of becoming "decisional," and to develop a document that would express our management philosophy and values while defining the arena in which future decisions would be made and the process by which the trust would make them.

The document we finally produced was closely linked to our procedures for environmental compliance (which we developed with the tireless assistance of the Council on Environmental Quality), but it was not an impact statement or even one of the other, lesser species of formal environmental analysis. It was a compromise and a good one. We called it our Framework and Strategic Guidance for Comprehensive Management, a name we shortened to Comprehensive Management Framework, or CMF for in-house use. We were just beginning to anticipate the relief of its completion when we were dealt a heavy blow.

Three members of the board were running out of time. Armstrong, Durkovich, and Stoddard had been appointed to two-year terms, the rest of us to four. The idea, common in board management and required by the Valles Caldera Preservation Act, was to stagger the terms of board members so that not all of them would expire at once. But we were at a critical juncture, and we could not afford to break up a board that was working together effectively. With the support of New Mexico's senators, we petitioned the White House to reappoint the three two-year members to new four-year terms. We argued that the reappointments were vital to the success of the experiment, and we were overjoyed when the White House agreed.

But then it didn't. Someone in the Office of Presidential Personnel noticed that Armstrong was a personal friend of Bill Clinton and a former high official of his administration. That would not do, we were told. President Bush would be unable to reappoint him, but we were assured that if Armstrong would voluntarily remove himself from consideration, the other two would receive the reappointment they and the trust desired. Although disappointed, Armstrong soon wrote a letter of resignation that is a model of easy wit and graciousness:

> December 17, 2002
>
> Dear Mr. President,
>
> I hereby tender my resignation from the Board of Directors of the Valles Caldera Trust.
>
> The Valles Caldera is truly a magic place. I hope you will visit it. It ranks up there with Yellowstone, Denali, and Yosemite; it's just on a smaller scale. The next time you are in Albuquerque or Los Alamos, get them to put it on your agenda.
>
> Sincerely yours,
>
> Bob Armstrong

For a second time, we thought we had a deal, but then we learned we didn't. In a routine check of donation records Presidential Personnel discovered that Durkovich and her husband had generously supported Democratic candidates, including President Bush's adversary, Al Gore, in the elections of 2000. That also would not do, we were told, and, accordingly, Durkovich would not be reappointed. Nor, for that matter, would Stoddard, notwithstanding that he was a staunch Republican, because it was now the policy of the administration—this was news to us and seemed to trump all previous communication—not to grant reappointments but to ensure that as many citizens as possible enjoyed an opportunity to serve their country. Irrespective of the trust's urgent need for stability, our fledgling organization would be getting three new board members.

It is no criticism of the three individuals who were later appointed to say that the White House's decision cost the board a serious loss of momentum. The new appointments were not made speedily. When they were made, the new members needed time to familiarize themselves with the preserve and its issues. And to varying degrees, in conscientiously exercising their responsibilities, they found themselves uncomfortable with certain of the board's previous decisions and insisted on reopening them. As a group we soon were plowing familiar ground anew in the CMF, as well as in other areas. As I had feared two years earlier when the Valles Caldera Preservation Act received its committee hearing, the relative importance of the trust's six management goals became the subject of repeated debate and reinterpretation. The prospect of moving on to major new undertakings, like transportation planning, which once had seemed so close, now receded into the distance.

LOOKING FORWARD

In the spring of 2004, the trust published its *Draft Comprehensive Management Framework*. The document described a vision for the preserve, at the center of which lay the lands of the caldera, which already possessed a high degree of ecological integrity. The trust promised to direct its stewardship toward achieving continued gains in ecosystem resilience and health while also producing for human benefit key commodities like grazing and a broad and accessible range of high-quality experiences. The trust would function in an open, consultative manner, following the streamlined procedures for environmental analysis that it had developed in cooperation with the Council on Environmental Quality. It would strive to optimize income and attain financial self-sufficiency, but it would not allow its pursuit of revenues to override its dedication to environmental protection and public service. The linchpin of the vision was the trust's dedication to science as a basis for sound, levelheaded decision making: the trust would monitor all major activities, measuring their ecological and, where possible, social impacts, and it would make the monitoring data it obtained openly available to the public. It would analyze these data in periodic reevaluations of its management strategies in a process widely known as "adaptive management," and it would regularly adjust and revise its strategies in light of what it learned from the monitoring data and other new information. The trust would function as a working ranch, but, in its broad commitment to the public and to the land, it would be more than that. Whether in the production of commodities or in the generation of valuable human experiences, it would strive, first and foremost, to produce learning.

These goals were—and are—both ambitious and attainable. In order to achieve them, the trust had to become a singular, top-quality professional institution. It had to attract and retain an outstanding staff fully committed to a corporate culture that emphasized initiative, openness to new learning, and communication with the public. It had to have a board of directors, secure in its supervisory role, which refrained from micromanagement or meddling, and which set an example for clarity of purpose and timely decision making.

Between the two great tasks facing the board of the Valles Caldera Trust—that of building the trust as a successful institution, and that of developing the policies and programs of the Valles Caldera National Preserve—the former has proved by far the more difficult but the latter has consistently monopolized the media's and the public's attention. The focus is understandable but unfortunate: an institution is a vehicle; what people want is the journey. Programs and even policies are visible and more easily evaluated. They also connect better with the stories people are predisposed to read in the unfolding saga of the trust. The most salient of these—and by far the most ideologically substantial—is whether livestock grazing or visitor activities will emerge as the predominant land use.[8] To be sure, this is an important issue, but it need not and should not be the central one. Skiers are

taught not to fix their gaze on the tree or rock that is the source of their danger. If they do (as I have done, too many times), the obstacle exerts a seemingly magnetic force and pulls them in to calamity. The trick is to focus elsewhere, to look not at the hazard but always at the path to safety. And then, in less than a heartbeat, the danger is passed.

This technique, which is effective in skiing, horseback riding, and other movement sports, can also work in politically charged arenas, including the management of public institutions, although it is not an easy tenet for many people to accept. For the Valles Caldera Trust, the path to safety involves operating openly and consultatively with the public, while relying on the nonideological lingua franca of unbiased monitoring data, both ecological and economic, to inform its discussions. It involves, above all, developing a stable institution of high integrity that is confident in the clarity and correctness of its mission.

By moving in this direction, the trust will best fulfill the dreams of its architects. The idea of a working ranch on public land was part of that vision. So was the goal of financial self-sufficiency. But precedent to both of these was the undergirding concept of a trust—a council of knowledgeable and dedicated citizens acting as a kind of mini-congress to chart the future of one of the great natural assets of the American landscape. This is a worthy, exciting, even noble experiment in land-management democracy, and its chief actors should think of it that way. The perils besetting the endeavor are many, and not least among them is the full Tolstoyan catalog of human frailty. No student of history or of current events can ignore the facility with which pettiness or egotism, or any of a number of character quirks, can derail undertakings of moment and purpose.

The management of the Valles Caldera Trust will be dynamic. As an institution it needs to experiment, and it needs to be free to alter its direction when alteration is clearly called for. At the same time, the greatest vulnerability of the trust—a vulnerability common to many public institutions in a representative democracy—is the constant turnover of its board, with roughly half of its appointed members being replaced every two years (and its ex officio members, for other reasons, changing as often). An added problem is the fact that the timing of appointments is roughly synchronous with the presidential election cycle, rendering the board susceptible to ideological swings— or abandonments—that undermine its established commitments. Under these circumstances, institutional memory can falter, as can the development of a durable and effective board culture. While adjustments of term length and the timing of appointments can mitigate such liabilities, goodwill and a decent respect for the labors of one's predecessors offer the best avenues for overcoming them—in fact, they are the only things that ever have.

CODA

The Valles Caldera is superlative in many respects but in no way more so than as a teaching landscape. Its lessons are everywhere accessible, and they are everywhere deeper and more complex than any of us is at first disposed to understand. And no one's understanding is ever complete. There is always more to appreciate, more to grasp, more nourishment to be had for mind and spirit.

You see, the caldera's potential is revealed in its geological and topographic character. It is not the largest caldera in the world nor even on the continent, but it is the best expressed, the most clearly and impressively discernible. If, as John Wesley Powell once said, the earth is a book of geologic history, its pages are nowhere more legible than at the Valles Caldera, where one can see etched in the landscape the power of more than a million years of volcanism and weathering. Another story eloquently told by the caldera concerns the resilience and durability of the land. The repeat photography included in this book (thanks to the kindness of Dr. Craig Allen of the U.S. Geological Survey) clearly documents the recovery of the land from earlier periods of overuse. These pairs of black-and-white images, which precisely duplicate the same view across the span of decades, tell us that this land has a history not unlike the history of a human life. It bears the scars of past experience and wears not a few wrinkles on its face. For all of this, the experiences it has to share are richer and the truths more layered than those proffered by the myth of the pristine.

As the land is dynamic, so is the story of the Valles Caldera Trust. The story is yet young and has far to go. It, too, has much to teach, and the worth of that teaching, along with the potential for success, will increase in proportion to the energy given to the project by an informed and caring public. Don Usner and I hope that this book may contribute toward that end. The Valles Caldera Trust represents the most audacious and significant experiment presently underway in the management of the public lands of the United States. It is a grand experiment in a grand place, made possible by the happy convergence of leadership and will at the highest levels of the national government. But while the preserve is a national asset and the trust is a federal entity, the undertaking that welds those two things into one is essentially local. The trustees are not a distant *them*. Most of them live and work nearby. If they do their work well, they will listen closely and often to what their neighbors tell them. They will listen no less attentively to those who travel long distances to experience the Valles Caldera. And if people who care about the caldera want the Valles Caldera National Preserve to be a place of inspiration and beauty, a place that offers excitement and wonder and that observes the highest standards of land stewardship, they need to say so to each successive group of trustees charged with the task of administering the Valles

Caldera Trust. The friends of the caldera need to repeat their message over and over and make sure that they are heard. If the preserve is to remain a place where eagles congregate in the fall and elk canter through the night like a living tissue of the land, the friends of the caldera need to insist on it, and settle for nothing less.

----

1. Craig Martin, *Valle Grande: A History of the Baca Location No. 1* (Los Alamos: All Seasons Publishing, 2003), 36–37. Another valuable source on the history of the grant and the uses to which it was put is Kurt F. Anschuetz and Thomas Merlan, "More Than a Scenic Mountain Landscape: Valles Caldera National Preserve Land-Use History," Rocky Mountain Research Station, USDA Forest Service, Albuquerque, September 2004. The history of the Pajarito Plateau and Bandelier National Monument is told in two works by Hal K. Rothman, *On Rims and Ridges: The Los Alamos Area since 1880* (Lincoln: University of Nebraska Press, 1992), and *Bandelier National Monument: An Administrative History*, Southwest Cultural Resources Center Professional Papers, No. 14 (Santa Fe: National Park Service, 1988).

2. "Remarks by the President to the Workers and Community of Los Alamos National Laboratory," February 3, 1998, issued by The White House, Office of the Press Secretary ([from] Albuquerque, New Mexico). N.B.: Clinton referred to the Baca as comprising 100,000 acres, but by this point in its history, sales, gifts, and trades of land had whittled down its size to about 95,000 acres.

3. "Statement by the Press Secretary: Agreement to Protect New Mexico's Scenic Baca Ranch," July 31, 1998, with two-page attachment, "Statement of Principles." Issued by The White House, Office of the Press Secretary ([from] The Hamptons, New York).

4. As quoted by Ian Hoffman, "Baca Ranch Deal Crumbles," *Albuquerque Journal North*, January 8, 1999, p. 3.

5. Members of such a team are usually anonymous, but here they deserve recognition for the job they did. Jack Craven, director of lands; Dave Sherman, coordinator of special projects; Paul Tittman, chief appraiser; Brent Handley, LWCF coordinator; and Denise McCaig, Baca coordinator for Region 3, all worked long and hard and impressively. Together with Janet Potts and Jim Snow, who are mentioned elsewhere in this essay, and many others, including Linda Lance of CEQ, who are not, they served the American people extremely well.

6. Ultimately, after allowing for Santa Clara's separate purchase of the headwaters of Santa Clara Creek, the federal government paid approximately $96.5 million for its share of the Baca Location.

7. Report [to accompany Senate Bill 1892], Valles Caldera Preservation Act, 106th Congress, Senate 2nd Session, 106–267, April 12, 2000, p. 5.

In a videotape recorded for distribution to board members of the Valles Caldera Trust, Senator Domenici summarized this point of view in his own words:

The act "also says at some point in time the land and its uses should yield some revenue and hopefully at some point in time the revenues might pay for the operation—no back expenses; you don't pick up years before. At some time it might be self-sufficient, but we were very careful there to say self-sufficiency isn't the only thing you are there to judge; you are also to judge how well we preserve it, how we maximize its use for recreation and other purposes. It's certainly not intended that it be a wilderness area or that we keep people off it. But in an orderly manner it should be used. It should be used for multiple purpose[s] and yield some revenue" ("The Acquisition of the Valles Caldera National Preserve," produced by the Woods Institute and N.A.K. Production Associates, 2001).

8. To say "visitor activities" is not just semantic hedging. It connotes a broad category of nonconsumptive uses that include such familiar forms of recreation as hiking, hunting, fishing, cross-country skiing, snowshoeing, camping, horseback riding, and sightseeing. But it can also reach beyond conventional notions of recreation to embrace archaeological and ecological field study, painting and photography workshops, planning and inspirational retreats, and many other forms of endeavor.

VALLE SANTA ROSA, 1906 AND 1997

This photo pair shows a view looking south from the terrace on the northeast side of Rio San Antonio. In 1906, a grove of young aspen trees occupied much of the slope at top center, evidence that a crown fire had burned part of the forest—probably at least twenty years earlier, given the few remaining snags. By 1997 the aspen stands were less abundant and smaller, as conifer species had increased in density and dominance, while blue spruce trees filled in the slopes above the stream. A century of fire suppression probably contributed a great deal to these conditions.

Overgrazing impacts are evident in the bottomlands in the 1906 photo. A substantial amount of rock is exposed along the terrace slopes. The rock is no longer evident in the 1997 photo, and the grasses on the valley floor appear healthier, showing increased biomass. The modern stream banks are more stable and rounded, having recovered from the trampling that left them bare and eroding in 1906. The stream channel width and meander pattern appear less pronounced in 1997, and exposed point bars are less prominent. The right foreground of the 1906 scene shows unvegetated areas (perhaps old stream meander scars) that are covered with footprints, likely reflecting livestock use. A fence line bisects the modern view, indicative of increased management of livestock grazing. (1906 photo, "Valle Santa Rosa at 8,500 ft. in Jemez Mtns." by Vernon Bailey, National Archives 22–WB–9007; 1997 photo, "JMFS 15," by Steve Tharnstrom and John Hogan; pair and caption information courtesy Craig D. Allen, USGS, Jemez Mtns. Field Station.)

VALLE SAN ANTONIO, 1906 AND 1997

This photo pair was taken looking northwest along Rio San Antonio. The photos show that between 1906 and 1997, forest density increased on the slopes in the middle distance, and conifers invaded meadow margins—blue spruce on the cooler, northeast-aspect slope at left, and ponderosa pine on the drier south-aspect slope at right. Forest density also increased on the distant slopes (center) and trees encroached into montane grasslands (on the skyline). Stream banks were unstable and eroding in 1906, with many rocks laid bare. Most of the rocks were hidden by soil and vegetation as the stream banks had recovered somewhat by 1997. The raw cut slope at right center in the 1997 photo is associated with a road. (1906 photo, "San Antonio Valley, Jemez Mountains, N.M.," by Vernon Bailey, National Archives 22–WB–9006;; 1997 photo, "JMFS 16," by Steve Tharnstrom and John Hogan; pair and caption information courtesy Craig D. Allen, USGS, Jemez Mtns. Field Station.)

VALLE GRANDE, 1935 AND 1997

These photographs were taken near the edge of the Valle Grande, looking southeast to the caldera rim peaks (Cerro Grande at the far left). The 1935 photograph shows sheep and cattle grazing, with a herder in attendance. A raw gully bank, visible behind the two foreground ponderosa pine (between the sheep and the cattle) in the 1935 photo, had largely healed by 1997. The large ponderosa pines present in 1935 were cut (note the stumps of the two foreground trees) and replaced by a cohort of young pines by 1997. The montane grassland atop Cerro Grande filled in with trees, and the forest edge advanced downslope into the Valle Grande. (1935 photo, "Sheep Grazing, Valle Grande, New Mexico," by T. Harmon Parkhurst, courtesy Museum of New Mexico, negative number 51462; 1997 photo, "JMFS 17(97)," by Steve Tharnstrom and John Hogan; pair and caption information courtesy Craig D. Allen, USGS, Jemez Mtns. Field Station.)

VALLE GRANDE, 1959 AND 1997

These photographs were taken from the eastern margin of the Valle Grande, looking northeast. The photo pair documents the rapidity of vegetation change in the caldera. In less than forty years, the extensive montane grasslands on the south slopes of Pajarito Mountain (partially blocked by the tree at right center in the 1956 view) and at Cañada Bonita (on the skyline in the center) diminished markedly in response to substantial tree invasion by Douglas fir, ponderosa pine, and Engelmann spruce. The photographs also illustrate a less dramatic downslope expansion of conifers into the fringes of the Valle Grande itself. A similar pattern of grassland contraction because of tree invasion, linked to a history of livestock grazing and fire suppression, has occurred throughout the Southwest. (1959 photo, "June 1959, Valle Grande," U.S. Department of Agriculture, Forest Service, negative number 491322; 1997 photo, "JMFS 19(97)," by Steve Tharnstrom and John Hogan; pair and caption information courtesy Craig D. Allen, USGS, Jemez Mtns. Field Station.)

Beyond the Fence:
A Legendary Landscape

Photographs and text by
DON J. USNER

Without a visual image, what meaning do things have? Photography's significance and importance lie therefore in its ability to convey visual information as well as to inspire a viewer to do something, like to think, feel or learn about life....Unless we know living things, how will we come to love them? Unless we learn to love them, we will not have the will to conserve, protect, or sustain them.—Carll Goodpasture[1]

Like many people growing up in northern New Mexico, in my youth I often visited the place in the Jemez Mountains now called the Valles Caldera. Memories of gazing across the fence, mingled with numerous stories about what lay beyond, wove about the caldera a powerful sense of place that captivates me to this day.

The tales I heard weren't the first to be told about the *valles*, the word the Spanish used to name the broad grassland valleys of the Jemez Mountains. For thousands of years Native people have lived in or vis-ited the Jemez and created narratives reflecting an elaborate, formal relationship with the mountains that is at once practical—they visit to hunt, gather food plants, trap eagles, and collect obsidian for tools—and profoundly spiritual, reaffirmed through ceremony and ritual. My bond with the valles of the Jemez began much more recently, when my father took me there and related his stories and those that he'd learned from other twentieth-century interlopers into the realm of the Jemez Mountain spirits. Early on, these experiences taught me to love the valles landscape. I remember well the first time I was smitten.

We were driving "up to the Jemez" in our '61 Plymouth station wagon. I stood in the middle of the front seat as we climbed up the snaking road, pausing to take in the open spaces at the Pajarito Plateau overlook and again to gaze into the richly forested depths of Frijoles Canyon. When we began to drop downhill through dark for-est, over the rim of the caldera, my father gestured out the window, saying, "There's the Valle Grande."

I saw it through the forest, a glowing expanse of golden light, broken in my view by the silhouettes of aspen trees. When we rounded the last bend of forest-lined road and broke into the spacious valle, stopping to stand by a pullout, my father tried to give me a sense of scale by pointing out specks that were cows and distant structures at the ranch headquarters, smaller than Monopoly houses. He talked about the first time he went out there, into the "Baca Ranch," that enormous acreage of private land whose name was even then layered with inviting connotations. He told of wandering from the roadside, leaving his car on the gravel road without worry about blocking traffic, and related his experiences of places accessible to him in years past but sequestered behind miles of barbed wire by the time I was a child. His words and the sudden awareness of that space and light sparked a sense of awe and anticipation that I've never forgotten.

Stories about what lay behind that fence in the Valle Grande, from numerous sources, multiplied throughout my youth—accounts (most apocryphal) of trout as long as a man's forearm, enormous deer, luxurious ranch buildings, bubbling hot springs, and more valles (bigger than the Valle Grande!) just out of sight. The tallest tales had the Valles Caldera as the largest one on earth, the remnant of a mountain 20,000 feet high that blew its top and threw rocks as big as boxcars clear to Kansas. We believed these fantastic tales because we had no information to contradict them.

In Chimayó, where I spent much time with my mother's Hispanic kin, the stories had a different timbre. For these farmers, mountains held the promise of water, that most valued of all elements in the arid valleys where they planted. Stockmen talked about the mountain pastures, nowhere as fabulous as in the valles that bore names their ancestors had given them—Valle Grande, Valle Toledo, Valle de los Posos, and more. My *tío* Nicasio Ortega told of getting permission from Frank Bond, the *patrón* who owned the Baca Ranch, to drive his wagon to the valles to gather firewood. Bond, a longtime New Mexico rancher, also owned mercantile stores in Española and large herds of sheep, and a few valley residents spoke of their experiences herding sheep—either their own or those belonging to "el Frank Bond"—in the valles. But for most, access to the fertile valles grasslands was prohibited, especially after the ranch sold in 1963 to a new *patrón*, whose roots lay in faraway Texas.

There was no shortage of stories about the "Valle Grande," the "Baca Location," or the "Baca Ranch"—all names we used for the off-limits property—but images were scarce. Since the late nineteenth century, photographs arguably have been as important as words for communicating a sense of place in the West. But for the Baca, most photographs available to the public were repetitious, taken from the same vantages along the highway. (My first photographs, taken when I was eight, fit in the highway category: grainy black-and-white pictures of the Plymouth, stopped by fence-deep snow in the blinding expanse of the Valle Grande.) Some powerful images were published by the Los Alamos newspaper to call attention to clear-cut logging on the property in the 1960s, and the few historic photos taken in the early twentieth century remained in archives away from public view (some of these are reproduced in this book). Harvey Caplin, well known for his photographs, photographed in the Baca Ranch, but his published pictures provided only tantalizing glimpses of the landscape.

In spite of—or perhaps because of—the dearth of printed images, the Valles Caldera loomed large in the imaginations of northern New Mexicans. We took pleasure in exploring around the edges of the Valle Grande, which is as far as most of us could get on foot, but we also felt cheated, denied firsthand knowledge of what was back in the other valles. We suffered a sense of helplessness, too, for even as we reveled in every opportunity to surreptitiously visit, we watched the land being pillaged by loggers who were carving roads into the forested mountains and hauling out ever-more trees. The prospect of large-scale geothermal energy development alarmed many nearby residents, especially the people of Jemez Pueblo, downstream from the many exploration wells already drilled. Counting specks in the tawny distances, we wondered how many more cows were out there in the unknown reaches of the ranch and what effect they were having on the land. The private ownership not only denied us access but also kept us from having a say in what happened in one of the most important parts of our world.

Thus it was with great delight that I first heard rumblings about public ownership of the Baca Ranch. These stirred from quiescence in the 1960s and grew stronger in the 1970s and 1980s as environ-

mental groups and the federal government tried to bring the ranch into the public domain. Much of northern New Mexico cheered when, in 1971, ranch owner James Patrick Dunigan managed to buy out the timber rights to the ranch (they had been severed from the land itself since 1918) and put an end to clear-cut logging, and a collective sigh of relief sounded again when in the mid-1980s an all-out effort by concerned citizens forced a utility company to scrap plans for a power line (the Ojo Line Extension) that would have run across the property. These efforts demonstrated just how strongly New Mexico residents felt about the Baca, even though it was not open to their entry.

Finally, in 2000, two years of negotiations—a history thoroughly chronicled in the essay by William deBuys in this book—led to an agreement on a price, and an act of Congress created the Valles Caldera National Preserve, making public for the first time the 88,900-acre property. The news made me, along with many other people, ecstatic.

My elation increased a few years later when the first board of trustees asked me to take photographs in the preserve. I took the assignment enthusiastically. The very prospect of having access into the old Baca Ranch brought me a thrill.

My task—to make photographs for public documents about the newly created preserve—seemed simple enough, but in practice the assignment proved challenging. The sheer size of the preserve, and the fact that I didn't know the lay of the land well, made it difficult to know where to begin. My image of the Valles Caldera had been built upon a fantasy. Those of us who grew up near the caldera had only rumors and legends laden with superlatives, and around these we constructed a hazy image of a vast landscape, replete with elk and practically unspoiled by human intrusion. Now, with a ranch road map in hand and a key to the gate, I was confronted with a large, rugged, many-faceted landscape.

The project began during the summer rainy season, when the valles is at its verdant peak. Each afternoon, drenching rain gave way to a sparkling sunset, and each morning dawned with fog and mist lifting from a resplendent green land. Striving to be present for the moments when sun crested and set on the caldera rim, I became a sleep-deprived, crepuscular creature. My exuberance—and a slumberous state of mind—made it difficult to grasp the reality of being there, but slowly, during that first summer and continuing periodic visits over the next three years, I began to feel out the physical dimensions of a place that was so large in my imagination that I could scarcely see it.

The practical aspects of getting around and making my way to remote vantages at dawn and dusk proved daunting, demanding long drives and hurried scrambles over rough terrain. Peculiarities of the valles landscape also presented challenges. Showing perspective in the valles, where distance is nearly impossible to gauge, is just one conundrum. The lighting in the caldera is often superb, sharp and clear or glowing from within rising mists, but the rim casts long shadows that make it difficult to capture soft morning and evening light. The elk, so compelling as subjects, stay just out of reach of a long camera lens; belly crawling for hours usually leads to a picture of retreating elk rumps in the distance.

In spite of the difficulties, with time photographs began to accumulate, each of them laden, for me, with memories of an experience behind the fence that I had longed for since childhood. The land exceeded even my imagined dimensions in its capacity to inspire. Wandering at all hours of the day and seasons of the year expanded my knowledge of the landscape while at the same time deepening my reverence for it. My exploration led me from the valles into old-growth forests of pine and fir, aspen groves, and a varied terrain of mountains, canyons, and cliffs. There were elk, to be sure, impressive and present at every turn, but also prairie dogs and bluebirds, ravens and ground squirrels, grasshoppers and meadowlarks, muskrats and eagles, and countless other animals living in the preserve.

Wherever I wandered in the caldera, the magnetism of the open valles tugged, drawing my attention back to those light-filled expanses. But I found equally compelling vistas from grassy summits of mountains and from the rock fields on their sides. From these vantages, the caldera fell into focus in the context of the surrounding terrain: the wide Pajarito Plateau, the deep gash of San Diego Canyon, the graceful summits of Caballo and Tsicoma.

When I began photographing, the extent of human impact—cow-trampled streambeds, cutover forests, dog-hair thickets, naked stump fields, hundreds of miles of hastily carved roads, drilling pads, fences, buildings, pipelines, and a small power line—surprised me. I tried at first to edit these out of every photograph, but with time spent on the land, many of these "blemishes" fell into place as part of the character of the Valles Caldera, telling not only of hard human use but also of the resilience of the land as well.

Awareness of new dimensions of the Valles Caldera grew from experience on the land and expanded through conversations with people—ranch hands, hunters, fishermen, Native Americans, scientists, land managers, artists, and hikers—whose visits overlapped my own. They showed me many ways to see the preserve: working ranch, sacred mountains, bountiful hunting preserve, recreational paradise, and field laboratory for archaeology, geology, and environmental and cultural history. The place is inherently complex, and diverse visions invest it with even greater intricacy.

The thrill of being in the Valles Caldera was increased by the joy of discovering a new place in the one I had imagined. The Baca Location of myth gave way to an even richer, more dynamic and diverse place of ever-deepening revelation.

When opportunities arose to present my photographs for public showing and I began to write captions, I found that simple titles or descriptions would not suffice. I struggled through fashioning tags that would provide some insight into the land as revealed in the photographs, but came up against a simple lack of published information. There were so many "firsts" unfolding in the new preserve, among them surveys of flora and fauna and detailed investigations of environmental history, archaeology, and geology, and few of these had published results.

Fortunately, while I was busy wandering the valles to make photographs, other people were actively gathering information about the landscape that could be shared. Craig Martin's superb history of the property was published the year I began photographing, as was a remarkable study of the vegetation by Esteban Muldavin and Phil Tonne. These provided useful information and insights, but for interpretations of specific features and processes revealed in the photographs I turned to Steve Reneau and Craig Allen, researchers who have devoted years to studying geological and ecological processes in the Jemez Mountains. When we sat down together and laid out the pictures, Reneau and Allen's passion for the Valles Caldera, and for their professions, poured out. Hours flew by as each picture evoked for them a revelatory story about the dynamics of the landscape. I

also called on Bill Zeedyk, a biologist with much experience in the preserve, for his insights and comments on stream photographs, and on writer Craig Martin for information on historic structures. Recast as extended captions in the pages to follow, comments from these people constitute an entirely different sort of story from those I grew up hearing—these grounded in a discipline of careful observation, but no less inspiring.

My intent in publishing this collection of photographs is not simply to share with others a glimpse of what lies "beyond the fence" in the preserve. The aim is also to engage people in a process of inquiry and discovery that leads to a passionate appreciation for this place, so long admired from afar. Most of all, I hope these photographs spark love for the landscape, as Carll Goodpasture suggests photographs can, and that this encourages others to seek out on-the-land experience and direct involvement in the stewardship experiment that is unfolding in the preserve. If public ownership means one thing, it's that those who cherish the valles landscape no longer need to stare across the fence, prohibited from experiencing what the land has to offer and powerless to shape what happens there. If there is broad public participation, the Valles Caldera's management experiment holds great hope for keeping the preserve a place that captures the imagination and touches the spirit for generations to come.

[1] Quoted in *Lenswork* 40 (April–May 2002): 85.

Valles Caldera

SOUTH MOUNTAIN AND THE VALLE GRANDE, 2005

The Valles Caldera, a depression thirteen miles across ringed by mountains, is the collapsed interior of a large volcano that erupted 1.2 million years ago. This aerial view looking north from 18,000 feet takes in the eastern half of the caldera, dominated by the tawny expanse of the Valle Grande, the largest of the caldera's broad, open grassland valleys (*valles*). The lumpy, rolling surface of South Mountain—the dark mountain mass in the foreground—hints at the volcanic origins of the Jemez Mountains. Especially prominent are the ripple-like pressure ridges on the mountain's eastern flank, showing the course of the lava as it flowed from the volcano's vent at the summit.

The South Mountain flow was the most recent of the large, mountain-building eruptions inside the Valles Caldera. It poured lava onto the surface of the caldera through faults that formed in a ring around the interior of the caldera after it collapsed—thus the designation "ring-fracture dome" for it and seven other, older domes in the caldera. When South Mountain erupted into the caldera 525,000 years ago, its lavas dammed the East Fork of the Jemez River, forming a very large, deep lake that filled the Valle Grande for perhaps 100,000 years. South Mountain Lake was neither the first lake, nor the last, to flood the Valle Grande. It drained when the river cut through a low spot between pressure ridges on the edge of the mountain.

MEANDERS ON THE EAST FORK OF THE JEMEZ RIVER IN THE VALLE GRANDE, 2005

The East Fork of the Jemez River meanders slowly across the Valle Grande as it cuts into river sediments and lake deposits. Abandoned meanders are visible alongside the present river course, along with a defunct diversion dam and the traces of an irrigation ditch. The irrigation works have altered the meander pattern, and one reach looks as if it was captured by an old wagon road or cattle trail.

Drill cores in this part of the Valle Grande have turned up lake-bed deposits 280 feet thick, laid down when South Mountain Lake filled the basin, and the upper elevation of the lake was probably 100 feet higher. Beneath the lake sediments, caldera fill, likely derived from streams, volcanic eruptions, and mass wasting deposits from the caldera walls, continues to an indeterminate depth. While exploring for groundwater sources for Los Alamos in the late 1940s, drillers encountered layers of sand and gravel and other unconsolidated fill down to 1,200 feet. They never hit bedrock.

VALLE GRANDE AND THE SIERRA DE LOS VALLES, 2003

Patches of golden aspens on the slopes of the Sierra de los Valles record the history of forest disturbance. Most of the large stand probably sprouted after the last major fire in this area, which ran through in the late nineteenth century. Since then, fire has been suppressed in the caldera, and Douglas fir, white fir, ponderosa pine, and other conifers have gradually grown up and are beginning to overtop and shade the aspens. Most aspen stands in the caldera are aging and being replaced through this process of natural succession. Carefully restoring fire to the Valles ecosystem would encourage new aspens to sprout, but they'd be unlikely to survive long, as today young aspen shoots in the caldera are almost universally consumed by elk. The future of aspen in the preserve depends on management of both elk and fire.

VALLE GRANDE, 2003

This view looking north across the northern end of the Valle Grande shows Cerro Rubio in sunlight on the horizon and Cerro del Medio on the left. Rounded boulders like those in the foreground lie around the outer edges of the valles where they have transported down from the walls of the caldera. Decreasing in size away from the rim, these rocks mark alluvial fans—tapering mounds of sediment washed off the rim slope over millennia. These particular rocks probably moved into place less than 50,000 years ago, since the alluvial fan that they rest upon bears no evidence of shoreline erosion from a lake that filled the Valle Grande then. Cavities in the rocks, formed by weathering after the rocks came to rest, provide drinking holes for small wildlife and habitat for aquatic insects and other small animals.

BOULDERS AND LIFTING FOG, VALLE GRANDE, 2003 (opposite)

These boulders on the edge of Cerro del Medio didn't tumble here from the caldera rim slope, like those in the photo this page. Instead, they mark the edge of the Cerro del Medio volcano, the oldest ring-fracture dome in the caldera, built up by lava from several distinctly different sources beginning about 1.2 million years ago—not long after the Valles Caldera itself formed. Woody shrubs, browsed heavily by elk in most of the preserve, thrive amid the rocks, where elk are reluctant to enter.

EAST FORK OF THE JEMEZ RIVER IN THE VALLE GRANDE, 2004

The East Fork of the Jemez River, near the main corrals of the old Baca Ranch, bears the marks of intensive livestock use in the recent past. Prior to public ownership of the caldera, ranchers gathered cattle in this area before shipping them off in trucks each fall. Chronic trampling caused the stream banks to collapse, broadening and widening the stream course and exposing the water to more sunlight, which raised the water temperature—conditions contrary to development of good native trout habitat. Fortunately, such damaged watercourses in the Valles Caldera can return to a healthier state if cattle are carefully managed. The stream here is already recovering, as sedges have moved in to colonize and rebuild the banks.

TWILIGHT POOL, EAST FORK OF THE JEMEZ RIVER, 2004

Although about half of the annual precipitation in the Jemez Mountains falls as rain in the summer "monsoon" season, winter snow is also critical for vegetation and wildlife. Melting snow soaks deeply and provides the much-needed steady runoff for early summer agriculture at lower elevations. In the caldera it also soaks dead wood and debris that could otherwise ignite easily and start wildfires during the dry early summer season.

From the late 1970s until the winter of 1995-96, snowfall in the caldera was relatively heavy, and the elk consistently moved out of the caldera, sometimes traveling all the way down to the Rio Grande and even across it. They grazed heavily in the ponderosa pine and piñon-juniper woodlands of the lower Pajarito Plateau, especially focusing on abundant forage there in the wake of the 1977 La Mesa fire. During most winters since 1996, though, snowfall has been relatively light, and the elk have rarely moved down below the mixed conifer forests. In some years, most of the elk have remained in the caldera all winter.

EAST FORK CANYON, 2005

There are few narrow canyons like this in the Valles Caldera. In all cases they have formed where watercourses cut through lava obstructions. The East Fork of the Jemez River carved this canyon when it eroded through the South Mountain lava dam, draining a large lake from the Valle Grande. Another dam formed 50,000 to 60,000 years ago, when the small El Cajete volcanic vent south of Redondo Peak spewed a great volume of pumice—a light, white volcanic rock. The deeply piled pumice blocked the East Fork, which once again filled the Valle Grande with water. This lake was short-lived, though; when the water level reached the top of the dam and started flowing over it, the dam probably failed almost instantaneously, likely unleashing an enormous flood in Jemez Canyon.

OLD-GROWTH PINES, VALLE GRANDE, 2005 (pages 70 and 72)

Old-growth ponderosa pine woodlands once fringed the relatively dry, south-facing slopes of all the valles in the Valles Caldera, but most of the pines were easy to access and were cut for lumber in the first half of the twentieth century. Ranch owners spared this stately grove, known locally as the History Grove, because they wanted to maintain the ambiance of the old forest in the vicinity of the ranch headquarters. The mature pines with the bright orange bark are two hundred to four hundred years old.

The trees grow well here on this east-facing slope of the Valle Grande because they stand on an alluvial fan of coarse, well-drained soils. The central part of the fan, where the alluvial soils are thicker and hold more water, supports Douglas fir and white fir along with the pines (page 72), but the drier margins of the fan support only pines (left). This grove of trees is an iconic example of what virgin pine forests looked like prior to the arrival of Europeans in the Southwest. There are very few such stands left in New Mexico, and of these, the History Grove may well be the largest. Virtually all other significant, accessible stands have been removed by logging.

In addition to logging, long-term suppression of fire has diminished the range of old-growth ponderosa pine in the Jemez Mountains. Before 1900, the grassy understory of old-growth stands was subject to frequent, widespread surface fires, which culled tree seedlings but rarely damaged adult trees. Without low-intensity fires to clear out small trees, old-growth stands become choked with undergrowth and vulnerable to intense, hot fires that can kill the adult trees. Catastrophic fires like the Cerro Grande fire of 2000, which burned just outside the Valles Caldera, have eliminated many old-growth pines in the Jemez and throughout the Southwest.

MIXED-CONIFER FOREST, SIERRA DE LOS VALLES, 2003 (opposite)

Nearly two-thirds of the forests on the preserve have been cut for timber, but some 25,000 acres remain untouched by logging. This forest on the western slope of the Sierra de los Valles adjoins large uncut tracts on nearby National Forest lands; together they make up the largest contiguous stand of virgin mixed-conifer forest remaining in the Jemez Mountains. Here, Douglas firs and white firs range in age from just sprouted to two hundred years old, indicating that regeneration is taking place and that surface fires have run through in the past. Patches of aspen indicate where hot fires or windfall took out large trees and opened up windows in the forest; young conifers sprouted in shadier sites where cooler, surface fires burned.

This stand of trees escaped logging because of its proximity to State Route 4, where logging would have been very visible. Loggers clear-cutting the forests in the 1960s concentrated first on stands out of sight from public roads, because by then the logging was controversial. The stand wraps around the east rim of the caldera and northward to Caballo Mountain. Such undisturbed mixed-conifer forest provides habitat for the Jemez Mountain salamander, endemic to the Jemez range.

LOGGING ROADS, SIERRA DE TOLEDO, 2005

Douglas fir, white fir, and other trees of the mixed-conifer forests on the caldera's mountainsides were most heavily targeted for logging after 1963, when construction of a mill in Arizona created a demand for pulpwood. This led to nearly a decade of intensive clear-cut logging and a frenzy of road building that created more than 1,000 miles of roads in the Baca Ranch. The roads led to widespread erosion and sedimentation of streams. Ranch owner James Patrick Dunigan bought the timber rights on his ranch and stopped the clear-cut logging in 1971. The roads in this photograph, wrapping around a summit in the Sierra de Toledo, mark the point in time when logging stopped. Here the roads were cut, but the trees were never felled.

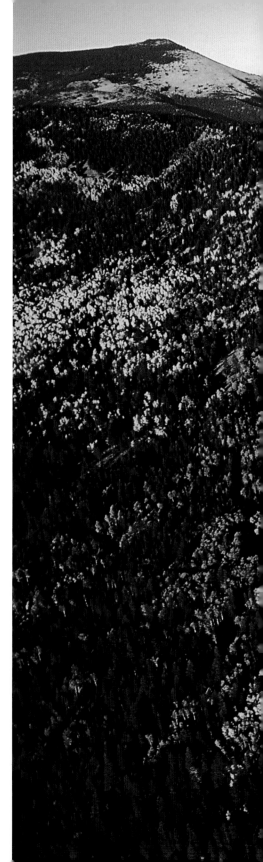

PONDEROSA PINE STUMPS, VALLE SAN ANTONIO, 2005

Forty thousand of the preserve's 65,000 acres of forested land have been harvested for timber. As a consequence, stump fields are a common sight. Here, on the edge of Valle San Antonio, native bunchgrass, once dominant across all of the caldera's grassland, grows along with sedges and Kentucky bluegrass in the spaces between ponderosa pine stumps, indicating that the area has been grazed fairly heavily by elk and cattle since the timber was harvested. Areas such as this on the forest/grassland margins experience some of the heaviest grazing in the caldera. Only the riparian bottoms along streams are grazed more intensively.

PONDEROSA PINE THICKET, VALLE GRANDE, 2003

This dense stand of ponderosa pine trees has taken over grassland on the edge of the Valle Grande. Similar dog-hair thickets also occur in many other places in the preserve. Fires, which ran through the valles grasslands regularly for centuries and typically spread through the pine forests, used to regularly thin out young pine trees. By reducing the biomass of the bunchgrasses that carry surface fire, intensive livestock grazing contributed to a decrease in fire frequency in the late nineteenth and early twentieth centuries—a problem exacerbated by concerted efforts on the part of ranchers and foresters to extinguish all fires. Without fire, young trees multiplied unchecked, creating thickets that consume much water and produce little forage for grazing animals. When especially dry, conifer thickets also create prime conditions for intense, hot wildfires that, unlike natural, low-intensity fires, cause great damage to vegetation and soils.

FELSENMEER, CERRO GRANDE, 2005

Felsenmeer (literally "sea of rock") refers to broken rock surfaces, usually found in high mountains and at high latitudes. Lava felsenmeers like this one on Cerro Grande are common on the rim of the Valles Caldera and on interior domes, especially on the resurgent dome of Redondo Peak. (The Spanish word for a scree slope is *derrubio*, and Cerro Rubio may be a corruption of *cerro derrubio*, a descriptive name for the large felsenmeer on Cerro Rubio's side.) Aspens grow on the margins of most felsenmeers in the Jemez, taking advantage of the plentiful sunlight in the rocky clearings. Aspens also may do well along felsenmeer margins because elk are reluctant to trod on the crazily uneven rock surface.

Much of the upper Jemez landform may have once looked like this felsenmeer. Although most of the rocky, volcanic terrain of the range is now masked by vegetation, the volcanic bones of the mountains remain underneath. In the felsenmeers' rocky mazes lives the Goat Peak pika, a subspecies of the American pika known only in the Jemez Mountains.

ASPENS, VALLE GRANDE, 2005

Aspen trees form an overstory only where fire or some other disturbance has cleared out other types of trees. These aspens, growing along the edge of the Valle Grande, took over when logging removed the conifer species (Douglas fir and ponderosa pine). As in almost all aspen stands in the preserve, the bark on the trees bears evidence of extensive elk browsing, and elk have consumed all young aspen shoots. Aspen bark is photosynthetic, and in late winter, when herbaceous vegetation has been long dormant, aspen bark is still nutritious. The elk break open the bark and make the trees susceptible to fungal infections.

VALLE SAN ANTONIO, 2005

The caldera moat—the space between the rim of the Valles Caldera and interior domes—defines Valle San Antonio. In this view looking east, the caldera rim is on the left, while the south side of the valle hugs the bases of San Antonio Mountain, Cerro Seco, Cerro San Luis, and Cerro Santa Rosa. Valle Toledo is visible at the base of the Sierra de los Posos and the east rim of the caldera. Rio San Antonio flows through the moat.

Lakes have filled the Valle San Antonio at least twice in the past million or so years, most recently—about 560,000 years ago—when lava flows from San Antonio Mountain reached the west rim of the caldera and closed off the exit for the watercourse. The lake backed up all the way into Valle Toledo, with fingers extending into Valle Santa Rosa and Valle San Luis, and then very slowly filled in with lake sediments and deposits from inflowing streams. Eventually water broke through the dam and the lake drained, leaving the river to wear its way through the sediments.

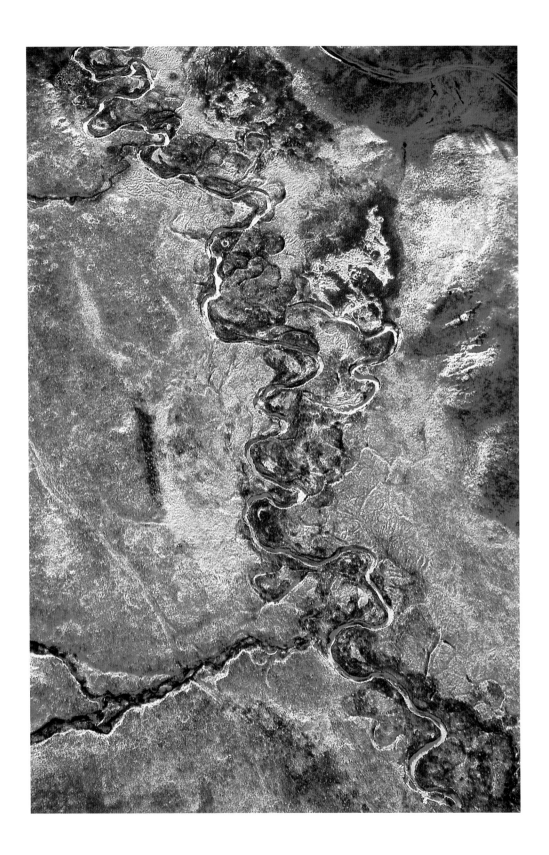

AERIAL PERSPECTIVE, RIO SAN ANTONIO, 2005

Rio San Antonio takes a sinuous path as it makes its way through the gently sloping Valle San Antonio. Abandoned meanders show past stream courses. One relatively straight stretch of stream seems to have been caused by cattle trailing along a fence line—its traces still apparent in the photo—that skirted the edge of the creek and crossed a meander. The trail could have captured floodwaters that, over time, incised a new path for the stream, shortening and steepening the channel and causing it to abandon the meander.

SAN ANTONIO MEANDERS, 2003

Here Rio San Antonio has cut through the northern edge of the Cerro Seco lava flow. A dense stand of blue spruce trees fringes the grasslands in the background. Such a fringe has become common on north-facing aspects bordering valles in the preserve. While blue spruce is a riparian species, its presence on these slopes, in dense stands, is a relatively new phenomenon. Grass fires burning from grasslands up into north aspects used to kill off colonizing trees, especially in dry years. One hundred years of fire suppression created a window for the spruce to colonize the slopes.

SAN ANTONIO SUNRISE, 2003

Wet meadows such as these at the junction of Rio San Antonio and Santa Rosa Creek can be found along the slowly meandering streams of the valles and near springs and seeps elsewhere in the preserve. These areas, where sedges, rushes, and some grasses thrive, become flooded, and their soils saturated, during spring runoff and again during the summer rainy season. In Alamo Canyon, persistent near-surface groundwater has led to the development of a fen—a wetland that is saturated year-round with water, in this case from warm springs. Most boggy areas located away from streams are ephemeral, coming and going wherever and whenever there's a relative abundance of water. The elk—especially bulls during the rut—find these spots and wallow in them, making mud holes.

In some places in the caldera, bogs lie just beneath the surface, making the ground undulate when trod upon—places locally referred to as "water beds." The tenuous, thin surface of terra firma can break underfoot. Ranch hands have found horses, cattle, and even elk stranded with their legs stuck in the soggy soil. Elk may even drown in the seemingly bottomless wet spots.

RIO SAN ANTONIO, 2003

One of the most striking things about the valles' watercourses is the lack of woody vegetation—particularly willows—along their banks. None of the few photographs available of the area from the early twentieth century show willows growing in the valles, indicating that the trees have been absent for a very long time. Perhaps they never grew in the fine-grained soils of the valles, but they do occur on well-drained soils along steeper stretches of creeks in the caldera, and a relic stand grows on the upper margins of Valle Seco. All of the existing stands are heavily browsed by elk, preventing willow reproduction. It may be that elk currently play a role in keeping the streams in the valles willow-free.

HERDING CATTLE, VALLE SAN ANTONIO, 2003

Spanish colonists introduced domestic livestock to northern New Mexico in the late sixteenth century, but the valles of the Jemez received only light and intermittent grazing use for the next two hundred years. Pueblo and Hispanic livestock owners were restricted in their use of these fabulous grazing lands because they were dangerous places, on the periphery of lands nominally controlled by Spanish authorities. Livestock fell prey to Navajos, who traveled through the Jemez routinely on raiding campaigns to the Rio Grande valley. Beginning in the mid-1800s, though, the valles became safer, and sheepherders began grazing tens of thousands of sheep in the valles each summer. Many were *partidarios*, who tended the sheep of a wealthy *patrón* in exchange for a share of the lambs born each year. After World War I, stockmen began a gradual shift from sheep to cattle, a change that was complete in the Valles Caldera by the 1960s. Since then, only cattle have been grazed in the valles, in numbers ranging from a few hundred to several thousand.

FOG, VALLE SAN ANTONIO, 2005

Fog lying low in the valles is a common sight. Because of its greater density, cold air collects beneath warmer, overlying air in the depressions of all the valles. Such temperature inversions occur almost daily, often causing moisture to condense and form fog. By killing off conifer seedlings, the cold air seems to be one of the primary factors that keeps the valles free of trees.

VALLE SANTA ROSA, 2003

(this page and opposite)
Logging eliminated a stand of large ponderosa pines on this low ridge at the juncture of Valle Santa Rosa and Valle San Antonio. Young trees are spreading downhill from an adult that was spared. In the background, a clearly delineated stream terrace rises to the forested slopes of Cerro San Luis. Large felsenmeers (rock fields) glow in the evening light on Redondo Peak in the distance. The young ponderosas probably lost their lower branches in a fire.

JARAMILLO CREEK, 2003

The banks of Jaramillo Creek overhang the small watercourse so much that the stream seems to disappear into grasses. It hasn't always looked this way. In 2000, when the Valles Caldera Trust took over the property, the creek looked much like the East Fork on page 65. The banks had been trampled by grazing animals and the creek flowed in a much broader, shallower channel. Stock were removed from the Valle Jaramillo that year and plants quickly recolonized the stream banks. By 2005, the creek in places had narrowed to less than half of its 2001 width.

The remarkable resilience of riparian areas in the preserve is due, in large measure, to the work of sedges, whose deep, fibrous root systems are extremely effective at holding fine-grained soil particles in place. Sedge rootlets collect soil particles and debris and bind them in place, gradually narrowing the stream channel in the process. Other plants then take hold to bind more soil and build up banks that eventually overhang the stream. Trout thrive in these conditions, finding shelter and shade beneath the banks. The shade also keeps creek temperatures cool, and invertebrates—especially grasshoppers—falling from the grasses provide a steady stream of food for the trout.

Cattle and elk are attracted to the young tips of sedge leaves because of their high protein content—about 22 percent. Removing cattle from the stream-bank area, or at least reducing the pressure by shortening the grazing period during the growing season, is essential to the recovery process.

REFLECTION IN RIO SAN ANTONIO, VALLE TOLEDO, 2003

The Valles Caldera is a wet place in an arid land—a giant, high-elevation bowl that captures and holds water. The plentiful water in the low parts of the valles makes the herbaceous vegetation resilient. Dry years slow down productivity, but deep rich soils, abundance of precipitation (relative to nearby lowlands), perennial streams, and near-surface groundwater make the overall system able to recover relatively quickly from drought and disturbance.

The Valles Caldera National Preserve includes within its boundaries the headwaters of several streams, including the East Fork of the Jemez River and Rio San Antonio—sources of water for many people downstream. This places the preserve management in the enviable position of controlling the caldera's watershed destiny, presenting opportunities that are absent in many other protected areas. It also means that residents downstream in the Rio Jemez watershed care a great deal about how the preserve is managed.

VALLE TOLEDO, 2005

In contrast to the well-worn, multiple terraces of the Valle San Antonio, the single, large river-cut terrace structure of Valle Toledo is sharp and fresh, suggesting a young age. Valle Toledo filled up with lake sediments beginning about 560,000 years ago, forming a large marsh that then filled from side to side with thick deposits of sand and gravel from inflowing streams. The coarse sediments hold water well: in the 1940s, drillers looking for a water supply for Los Alamos struck pressurized water in the middle of the Valle Toledo. The resulting artesian wells are still flowing, contributing significantly to the volume of the Rio San Antonio. (Similarly, some wells in the middle of the Valle Grande leak water to the East Fork, on a much smaller scale.)

VALLE DE LOS POSOS, 1985 (this page and opposite)

Valle de los Posos nestles in the rolling mountains called the Cerros de los Posos. *Posos* (more formally spelled *pozos*) means "deep holes," "wells," or "graves." Here the name refers to the presence of unusual, shallow depressions in this valle. The Cerros de los Posos rose after an explosive eruption in the Jemez range that formed the Toledo Caldera, 400,000 years before the larger Valles Caldera formed. The more recent Valles Caldera collapsed over and buried the Toledo Caldera, which had collapsed over an older, smaller caldera. The Cerros de los Posos may have emerged as ring-fracture domes inside the Toledo Caldera.

VIEW FROM REDONDITO, 2005

Not all of the interior of the Valles Caldera is dominated by the grassland bowls of valles. Extensive conifer forests dominate the interior cerros and the ridges of the Redondo Border, dominant in this view looking north from a felsenmeer on Redondito. These ridges formed as the resurgent dome of Redondo Mountain uplifted from the caldera, pushing up surrounding blocks of rock. The uplifted rocks of the Redondo Border include young volcanic rocks and caldera fill.

FENCE LINE, VALLE SAN ANTONIO, 2005

The Redondo Development Company began fencing the perimeter of the Baca Ranch in 1918 as a bold move to bolster its claim that a U.S. government survey had cheated it out of 8,000 acres of land. The hand-hewn wood posts of this fence in the Valle San Antonio were put in place later, probably when the nearby San Antonio Cabin was built in the late 1940s. Before then, there was little need for interior fences, as sheep ranchers, dominant here in the first half of the twentieth century, relied upon shepherds and herd dogs to contain their animals. Since the 1940s, the grasslands have been divided into pastures—twenty in all—comprising nearly 43,000 acres of fenced land for managing cattle and horses. The Valle San Antonio and the Valle Grande have been divided most extensively, while the Toledo remains largely fence-free.

Fences may be contributing to a loss of elk calves in the preserve, as calves cannot easily cross fences and, as a consequence, often become stranded from their mothers and highly susceptible to predation.

BARN AND CORRAL, VALLE GRANDE, 2003

Although no one knows for sure when this barn was built, the construction technique and the condition of the logs suggest it is one of the oldest standing buildings on the preserve. The Dunigans called the structure, located in the Valle Grande near ranch headquarters, the Salt Barn. It may have been built when Mariano S. Otero and his son owned the ranch around the turn of the twentieth century.

NATURAL GAS PIPELINE ROAD AND SHACK,
VALLE SAN ANTONIO, 2005 (this page and opposite)
This road and pump shack sit over a natural gas pipeline
laid across the Valle San Antonio and Valle Toledo in the
1940s. The line delivers gas from the San Juan basin to
Los Alamos. In places, the pipeline road is washing out—
just one of many roadways in the preserve, many of them
abandoned, that are creating erosion and contributing to
stream sedimentation. Although well over a thousand
miles of road have been built on the property, only about
140 miles remain open to vehicular access now.

ABANDONED BEAVER DAMS, RITO DE LOS INDIOS, 2005

Until recently, beaver inhabited this small tributary of Rio San Antonio, as well as Sulfur Creek and creeks on the west side of Redondo Peak. Their most recent dam building lies against an earlier generation of beaver works, now filled with sediments and anchored by a solid cover of vegetation. The beaver have been gone for at least a few decades, their ingenious engineering now laid bare. The reasons for their departure remain unclear, but the tree species that beaver depend on for food—aspen, willow, and other riparian vegetation—are completely absent within several hundred feet of the dams. Reestablishing beaver in the preserve could help restore riparian areas and create fish habitat, but, on Rito de los Indios at least, reintroduction might be futile, since the beavers' food source is gone.

Beavers are not the only animals that have been eliminated from the caldera in the past 100 years. Wolves, grizzly bears, and perhaps river otters, mink, and martens also once lived here but are now absent. Even more recently, since the 1970s, leopard frogs have disappeared from the entire Jemez Mountain range, for unknown reasons.

CERRO DE LA GARITA, 2003

Montane grasslands like these on the north rim of the caldera grow on the upper margins of steep south- or southwest-facing slopes of the preserve, forming clearings in the mixed-conifer and the spruce/fir forests. The soils underneath, essentially prairie soils, extend very deep, indicating that grasslands have grown on these sites for thousands of years. These are the most productive grasslands in New Mexico in terms of biomass production, and, because they're on steep slopes far from perennial water sources, over the past fifty years they've received much lighter cattle grazing than lower grasslands in the valles.

Fire is largely responsible for maintaining these islands of grassland. Fire scars from trees on the grassland margins indicate that southerly aspects in the Jemez burned, even at high elevations, on the order of every ten years. However, if trees can make it to fifteen or twenty years old here, they can survive grass fires and grow fast in the deep soils. With widespread suppression of fire for the past century, this is exactly what has happened on the grassland ridges of the preserve. Without fire, conifers and aspens have taken over large areas of montane grassland.

CERRO GRANDE, 2005

These montane grasslands on the summit of Cerro Grande have a similar origin to those on page 115, but here the soils are shallower and a number of shrubs grow amid the grasses. Photographs from the early 1980s show that the shrubs were once much taller. Since then, the shrubs have been grazed heavily by elk, leaving them cropped and stunted. Except in rocky areas and other rough terrain, there is almost no young, woody, deciduous vegetation in the caldera that has escaped the elk.

Cerro Grande is a name now associated with the infamous Cerro Grande fire, which burned more than 40,000 acres and hundreds of homes in nearby Los Alamos in May of 2000. The fire started near the summit of the mountain, but did not burn intensely there. The mountaintop offers sweeping views across Bandelier National Monument, whose canyons bisect layers of volcanic rock that flowed from eruptions in the Valles Caldera 1.2 million years ago. The layers comprise a vast apron of volcanic ash that spread toward the distant Rio Grande in spectacular, pyroclastic flows, solidifying into light, porous rock called tuff. Here the tuff reaches 800 feet in thickness—the thickest Bandelier Tuff on the Pajarito Plateau. Riddled with natural caves formed by weathering, the tuff offered a convenient place for prehistoric people to construct cliff dwellings, now included in Bandelier National Monument.

BUNCHGRASS, VALLE GRANDE, 2003

Bunchgrass-dominated montane grasslands like these grow on the well-drained parts of all the valles. Together with the grasslands on south-facing summits, they cover more than one-fourth of the preserve—about 26,000 acres—comprising one of the largest montane grassland areas in the Southern Rocky Mountains region. Few such grasslands in the Southwest are protected from overgrazing, development, or other impacts. The grasslands of the preserve are rare and important for their size and their relatively good condition, although they have suffered considerable impact. Because of grazing and fire suppression, trees are encroaching on grasslands in many of the valles. The encroachment may also be indicative of a warming climate.

ROCKY MOUNTAIN ELK (2003, 2004, 2005) (pages 120-125)

Three to four thousand elk—about 75 percent of the Jemez Mountain population—now live in the Valles Caldera in the summer months, yet elk bones are very rare in archaeological sites in and around the Jemez Mountains, suggesting that the Valles Caldera has not supported elk in such large numbers for a long time, if ever. Pressure from aboriginal hunters may have kept elk numbers low for much of the past thousand years, since the Jemez range was encircled throughout that time by a population of several thousand people. As snow forced elk out of the high country in heavy snow years and they dispersed into the region where human population was concentrated, hunters may have killed enough animals to reduce the elk population and keep it from rebounding.

After the arrival of Europeans, elk were hunted to extinction in the Jemez by the late nineteenth century. All the elk in the mountain range derive from small herds introduced from Wyoming in the 1947 and again in 1964, and they've multiplied dramatically. Their abundance in the preserve now is subjecting vegetation to intense herbivory. The effects of elk browsing have become widespread and marked, in part because elk, although stereotyped as grazers, eat such a broad spectrum of plant life.

The effects of elk grazing are especially evident in dry years. In 2002, June was so dry that the only green vegetation visible in the valles grasslands lined riparian zones in narrow ribbons. The elk concentrated there because of the nutritious forage, and had a tremendous impact on the vegetation. Elk also have almost completely shut down aspen reproduction in the preserve by eating young aspen shoots.

The elk may be feeling the effects of their overuse of the habitat: the calf recruitment rate—the survival rate for newborns—has been low in recent years, and the problem may be nutritional, at least in part. Elk browsing is especially intense in the caldera during dry years, when the elk don't leave for most or all of the winter. They browse the woody vegetation especially hard in the lean months of late winter and early spring, leaving little for the lean spring months when pregnant cows need nutrition most.

KESTREL, VALLE GRANDE, 2004

Kestrels, red-tailed hawks, and turkey vultures are the most common birds of prey in the Valles Caldera. Bald eagles pause in the preserve during their fall migration—forming the largest fall concentration of bald eagles in New Mexico—perching on snags near creeks and consuming fish, prairie dogs, or carrion, including elk entrails left by hunters. Golden eagles live there spring through fall, until prairie dogs, their favored food, retreat beneath ground for the winter. Goshawks haunt the preserve's old-growth forests and may breed there. All told, nearly one hundred species of birds breed in the preserve.